SKILL SHARPENERS STEAM

Keep Your Child's Academic Skills Sharp

2

This book belongs to

name

Contents

Full STEAM Ahead!

Science, **Technology**, **Engineering**, **Art**, and **Math** activities, or **STEAM** activities, help you learn about problems that need to be solved. **STEAM** activities help you think about how someone with that problem may feel. They also help you think about what you can do to solve the problem.

You can use what you know or what you will learn about **Science**, **Technology**, **Engineering**, **Art**, and **Math** to find solutions. There is not one answer or one solution to a problem. You can come up with an idea and see if it works. If it doesn't, you can try again. You should feel good about what you make and the ideas you have whether they work or not. **STEAM** is about being creative and trying to find solutions.

So, let's have fun and go
full STEAM ahead
into solving real-world problems!

General Materials List

- pencil
- paper bag
- aluminum foil
- glue
- tape

- glitter
- markers
- colored pencils
- crayons

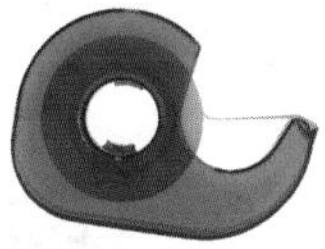

- construction paper
- sheets of white paper
- string or shoelace
- hole punch
- feathers

- stickers
- pompoms
- cardboard
- duct tape

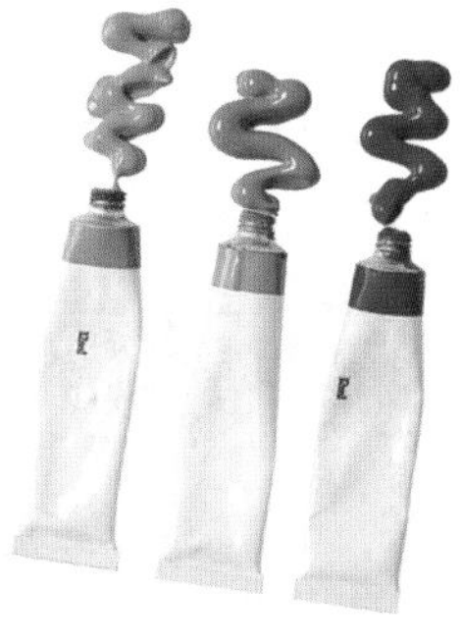

- paint
- paintbrush
- sponge
- newspaper

- cotton balls
- stapler
- laptop, phone, or other device that can play music and record videos
- dance party ball or mirrored ball

- scissors
- different colored yarn
- twine
- rubber bands
- people to act in a play
- foods such as bread, berries, carrots, bananas, corn, cucumbers
- jump rope

- plastic cups
- hula hoop
- shoebox or backpack

Concepts:
Roads need to be safe for both cyclists and motorists;
Making bike lanes safer might encourage more people to ride bikes

Safe Bike Lanes

Read the story. Think about the problems in the story.

On the Way to Soccer

Jalisa was getting ready for soccer practice. She put on her special soccer shoes while her dad watched the news on TV. "There will be lots of cars on the road today for the carnival. It may take you longer to get places," said the lady on TV.

"Oh no, Dad, how can we get to practice without getting stuck in traffic?" asked Jalisa.

"We can ride our bikes!" said Dad. So Jalisa rode her bike on the sidewalk while Dad rode in the bike lane in the road. Suddenly, a car drove too close to Dad. This scared Dad and made him fall off his bike. Luckily, he was not hurt, but this made Jalisa think. "Bike lanes need to be safer so cars do not hit bike riders."

After practice, Jalisa wrote a letter to the city to ask them to make safer bike lanes. The city thought it was a good idea. Soon, they put pavement and big boxes of flowers in between the bike lane and the car lanes. Now the cars were far away from the bike lane and it was much safer for all bike riders.

Problems on the Way to Soccer

Skills:
Identify key problems and ideas in a text;
Summarize a problem;
Formulate a solution to problems;
Produce a creative drawing to interpret a problem

Answer the items about the story you read.

1. Draw a picture of one problem you read about in the story. Then write a sentence about it.

One problem in the story is ______________________________

____.

2. How was the problem fixed?

This problem was fixed when ______________________________

____.

3. What is another way to fix the problem?

Another way to fix the problem is ______________________________

____.

Safer Bike Rides

Bike riding is fun. It is a great way to exercise. It is also good for the environment. But sadly, some people get hurt riding bikes.

Bike Lanes

More and more people are choosing to ride their bikes to get places. So towns have bike lanes. A bike lane is a path in the road that is only for bike riders. A thick line is painted in between the bike and car lanes. Bike lanes also have a picture of a bike or the words **Bike Lane** painted in the lane to let people know where they can ride safely. People 10 years of age or older can ride in the bike lane.

Concepts:
Bike lanes can help make roads safe for both cyclists and motorists;
There are ways to make bike lanes even safer;
Bike lanes have certain features that make them user-friendly

Safe Bike Lanes

Why Bike Lanes Are Important

Bike lanes are important because they keep bike riders and all other people safe. Before bike lanes, people rode on the sidewalk or in the same lanes as the cars on the street. Riding a bike on the sidewalk can cause you to crash into someone who is walking by. And riding a bike in the same lanes as cars can be unsafe, too. Bikes move more slowly than cars, so people driving behind bikes will try to go around them. These cars could hit the bike riders or other cars.

Safer Bike Lanes

Even though bike lanes are helpful, people on bikes are still getting hurt. This is mostly because cars travel too close to bike riders. This is why towns are making new bike lanes. Some towns paint the bike lanes bright blue, green, or red to help drivers see the bike path more easily. Some people believe there are even more ways to make bike lanes safer.

Skills:

Use visual art and creativity to serve a purpose;

Explore uses of materials and tools to create works of art or design;

Use observation and investigation in preparation for making a work of art;

Demonstrate creativity

Safety Vest

Sometimes, people driving in cars have a hard time seeing bike riders. One way bike riders can stay safe is to wear a safety vest. A safety vest is a bright vest that helps others see you better.

Make a bright safety vest that will help you stay safe when you ride a bike.

Step 1: Brainstorm

- Think about who will wear the vest and why.
- Think about how the different parts of the vest keep people safe.

Step 2: Do Research

This picture shows a safety vest.

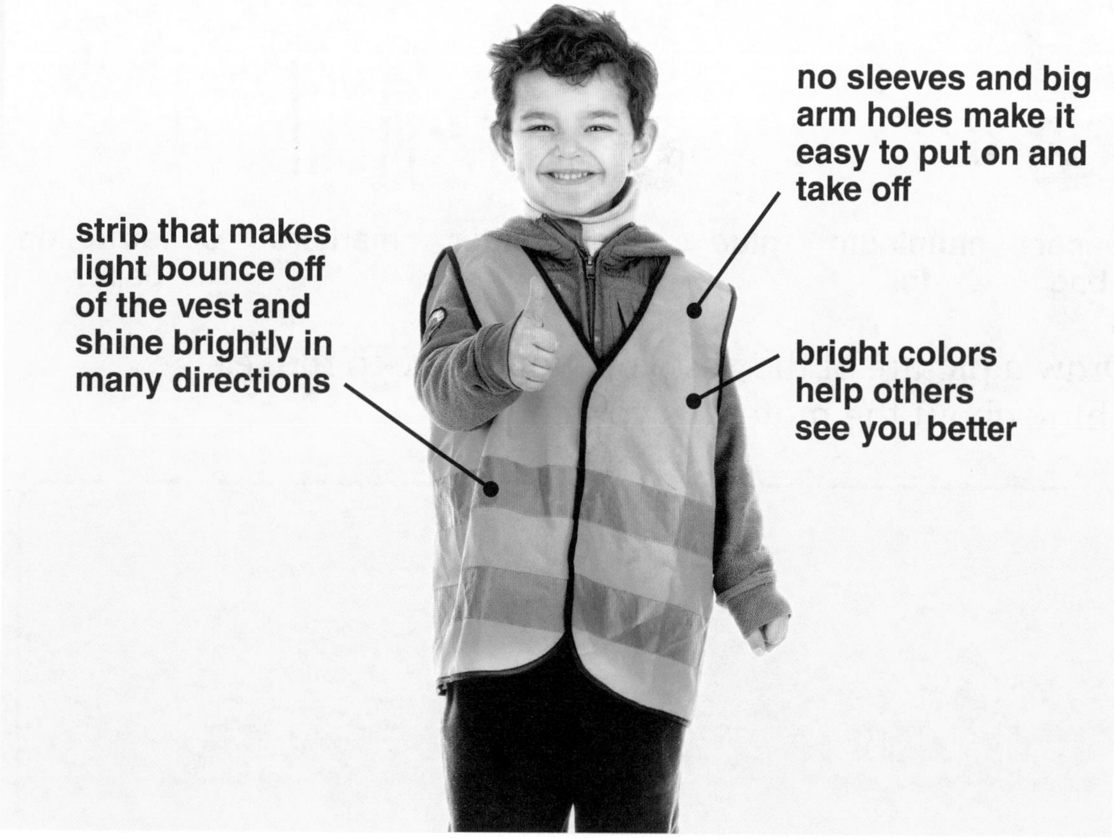

Think about these questions as you look at the picture:

- What color is the vest, and why does it matter?
- How does the vest help people see you?
- Why is it important for the vest to have big arm holes?
- Why should the vest be easy to take on and off?

Step 3: Plan

Choose the things you want to use.
Things you might use:

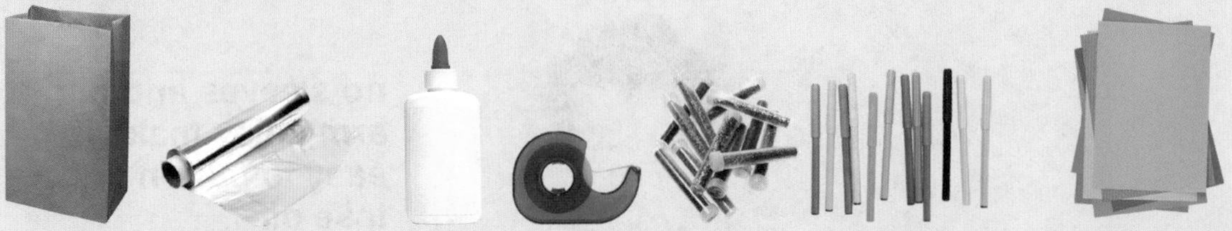

paper bag | aluminum foil | glue | tape | glitter | markers | construction paper

Draw a picture of the vest you would like to make.
Think about the materials you chose.

Step 4: Make It and Share It

Make your vest. Then show it to a friend.
Tell your friend why you made it.

Bike Lane Requirements

People who make bike lanes use math. Bike lanes in the United States must be at least 3 feet wide.

Skills:
Subtract within 20;
Relate subtraction to length;
Use a number line diagram;
Apply a mathematical concept to formulate a logical answer

Write the width of the lanes. Then answer the items.

1. _____ feet

2. _____ feet

3. How much wider is lane B than lane A?

Lane B is _____ feet wider.

4. Which bike lane would be safer to ride in? Why?

____

____

Skills:

Learn about features and tools used to construct traffic lanes;

Identify road technology features;

Match pictures to descriptions

Road Safety Technology

Technology helps people stay safe on the road. Islands, reflectors, and rumble strips help people stay in their lanes. Road signs tell you where to go and what to do.

Draw lines to match.

- a wall or grassy area placed in between lanes
- words and pictures that tell you what to do on the roads
- small shiny objects in between lanes that light bounces off of
- rows of raised strips on the edge of car lanes that make a loud rumbling sound when tires roll on top of them

Highway Engineer

Highway engineers are people who design roads, bridges, and tunnels. They decide which road safety technology is best to place on the roads to keep people safe.

Skills:

Use visual information and informational text to draw a conclusion;

Learn about how highway engineers design things to make traveling safer

Read. Then choose an item from the box to make the street safe. Write it on the line to finish the sentence.

Puja needs to cross the street to get to school. But the cars will not stop for her. Which of these should the engineer build to help Puja cross the busy street?

stop sign **rumble strip**

The ____________________ will help Puja cross the street.

Skills:
Problem solving;
Creative skills;
Solving problem-based, authentic tasks;
Connected ideas

Problem to Solve

Many bike riders in your town have been getting hurt because of cars that drive into bike lanes. The town needs safer bike lanes. You will design a safer bike lane for your town.

Task

First, do the research on the next page. Then brainstorm and design on page 18. Last, draw your final design for a safer bike lane on page 19.

Rule

- Bikes in the bike lane must travel in the same direction as traffic, or in the same direction cars are driving.

Things you might use

A Bright Path

Read. Look at the picture. Then answer the items.

This bike lane in Canada was painted green. The bright color helps people who are driving in cars see the bike lane more clearly.

1. How did this city in Canada make the bike lane safer to ride in?

____

2. Do you think this bike lane could be made even safer? Tell why or why not.

____

____

Skills:
Conduct research;
Use visual information;
Hypothesize;
Answer questions based on visual information

Problem & Task → Research → **Brainstorm & Design** → Make It & Explain It

Skills:

Use concepts to solve a non-routine problem;

Apply concepts;

Design a safe bike lane;

Create a solution to a problem;

Brainstorm ideas for a creative design;

Use creativity

Bike Lane Brainstorm

Answer the items to help you brainstorm ideas for your safe bike lane.

1. What is one way bike riders get hurt when riding in the bike lanes on the street?

____

____

2. What are some ways to make sure that people driving in cars can see bike riders?

____

____

3. There are many ways to design a safe bike lane. Draw two different designs for your bike lane.

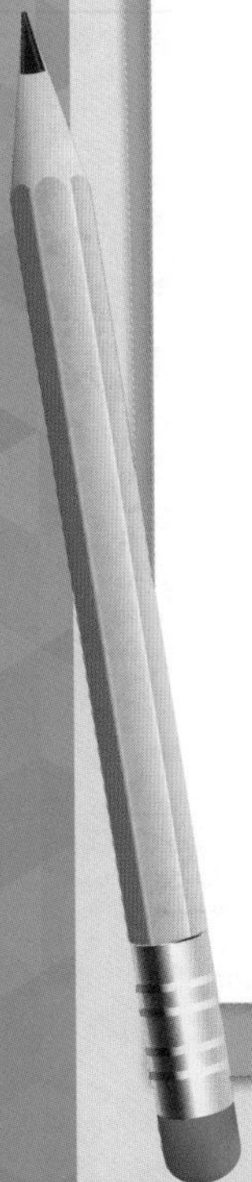

My Safe Bike Lane

Choose the bike lane design you like best. Draw the final design in the box below. Then tell how your design will help make bike lanes safer.

My design will make bike lanes safer because ______________________

____

____

____

____.

Skills:

Explain a design;

Draw a final draft of a creative design;

Explain the function of the features of a bike lane;

Draw or present visual information;

Evaluate a design

Concepts:
Some children are not able to get shoes that fit;
Having shoes that fit and are comfortable is important for health and safety;
Some people donate old shoes to other people

Read the story. Think about the problems in the story.

Shoes for Katya

Katya grabbed her shoes by the front door. "I hope I can get my feet inside them this time," Katya thought to herself. Her old shoes were too small for her feet. There were small holes on the sides of the shoes, too. But her family did not have money to buy new shoes. This is the only pair she owns. As Katya squeezed her feet into the shoes, the small holes tore

open. Her toes popped out of the shoes! Katya frowned. She did not want to walk with her toes out, but she knew she did not have money to buy new shoes. "Hmm…what can I do?" thought Katya. She found some tape and wrapped it around the shoes. "Perfect, now there are no more holes!" Katya put on her backpack and walked to school.

Just as Katya reached her school, she hit her toes on a sharp rock. "Ouch! That hurt!" Katya looked down at her shoes and saw the taped had ripped off. She also had a cut on her toe.

Her teacher saw her and said, "Let's clean your toe and get you a pair of shoes. Some kids did not need their shoes anymore, so they gave them to the school for students." Katya smiled. She was so happy to get a new pair of shoes.

Holey Shoes

Skills:
Identify key problems and ideas in a text;
Summarize a problem;
Formulate a solution to a problem;
Produce a creative drawing to interpret a problem

Answer the items about the story you read.

1. Draw a picture of one problem you read about in the story. Then write a sentence about it.

One problem in the story is ______________________________

____.

2. How was the problem fixed?

This problem was fixed when ______________________________

____.

3. What is another way to fix the problem?

Another way to fix the problem is ______________________________

____.

Shoes

Every child needs shoes. Shoes help protect your feet and keep your body healthy. But did you know that many children around the world do not have shoes?

© Claudio Soldi / Shutterstock.com

Walking Without Shoes

Every day, children walk to school and other places with no shoes on their feet. They walk over dirt, rocks, and sharp objects. These things can hurt your feet and make you sick.

© Anton_Ivanov / Shutterstock.com

On a snowy day, you can walk to school with boots that will protect you from the cold, wet snow. But can you imagine walking to school in the snow without shoes? Many children have to miss school because they do not have the shoes to protect them from snow or other weather.

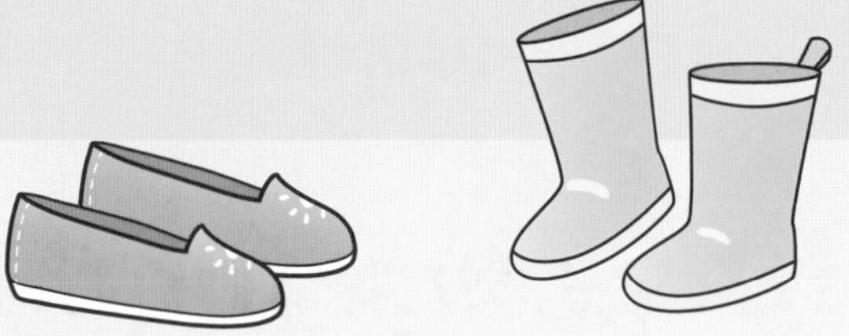

Why Shoes Are Important

Shoes are important because they protect your feet. Shoes are also important because they help you do the things you love.

Like playing a sport,

exploring the outdoors,

Or staying comfy in your home.

How You Can Help

Our feet change sizes because they grow. When this happens, we need to buy new shoes that fit our feet. Instead of throwing away your old shoes, give them to someone in need. You can brighten someone's day and change their life.

Concepts:
Shoes protect our feet and help keep us healthy and safe;
Some children do not have access to shoes that fit;
People's feet change, and children grow out of old shoes;
Some people donate shoes to other people in need

Shoes for All

Skills:
Convey an idea through visual art;
Explore uses of materials and tools to create works of art or design;
Demonstrate creativity

Shoes Just for Me

Shoes are designed for many different reasons. Some shoes are designed so people can show what they like and what makes them feel special.

Design a pair of shoes to show what makes you feel special.

What You Need

- cutout on page 25
- string or shoelace
- hole punch
- tape
- markers or colored pencils
- Optional: feathers, glitter, stickers, pompoms, etc.

What You Do

1. Cut out the shoe on page 25 and hole punch the gray circles.
2. Decorate the shoe with markers, colored pencils, stickers, and any other items to tell more about what you like and what makes you feel special.
3. Last, tape one end of the string or shoelace to the back of the shoe. Then thread the other end through the holes and tie a bow.

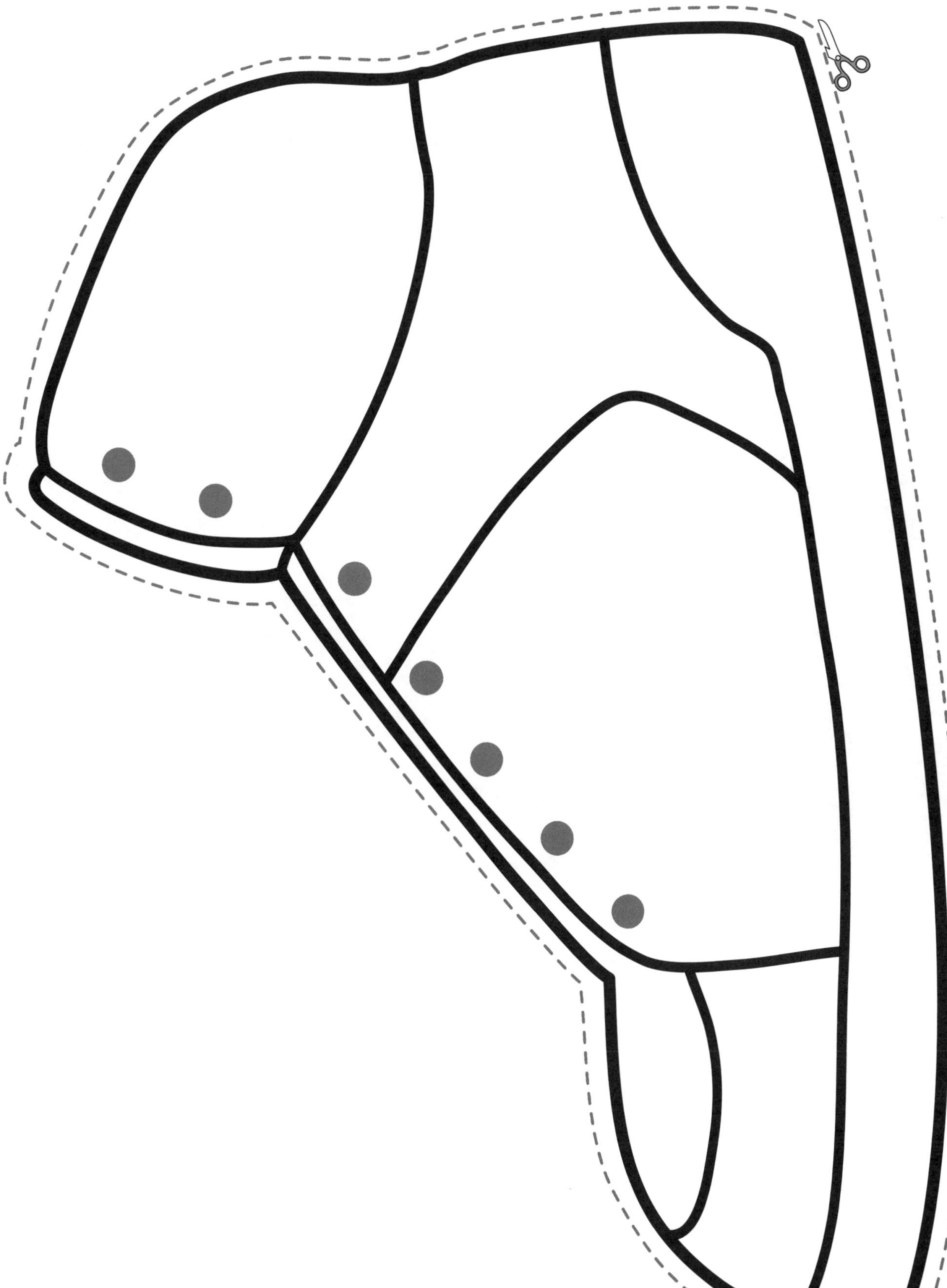

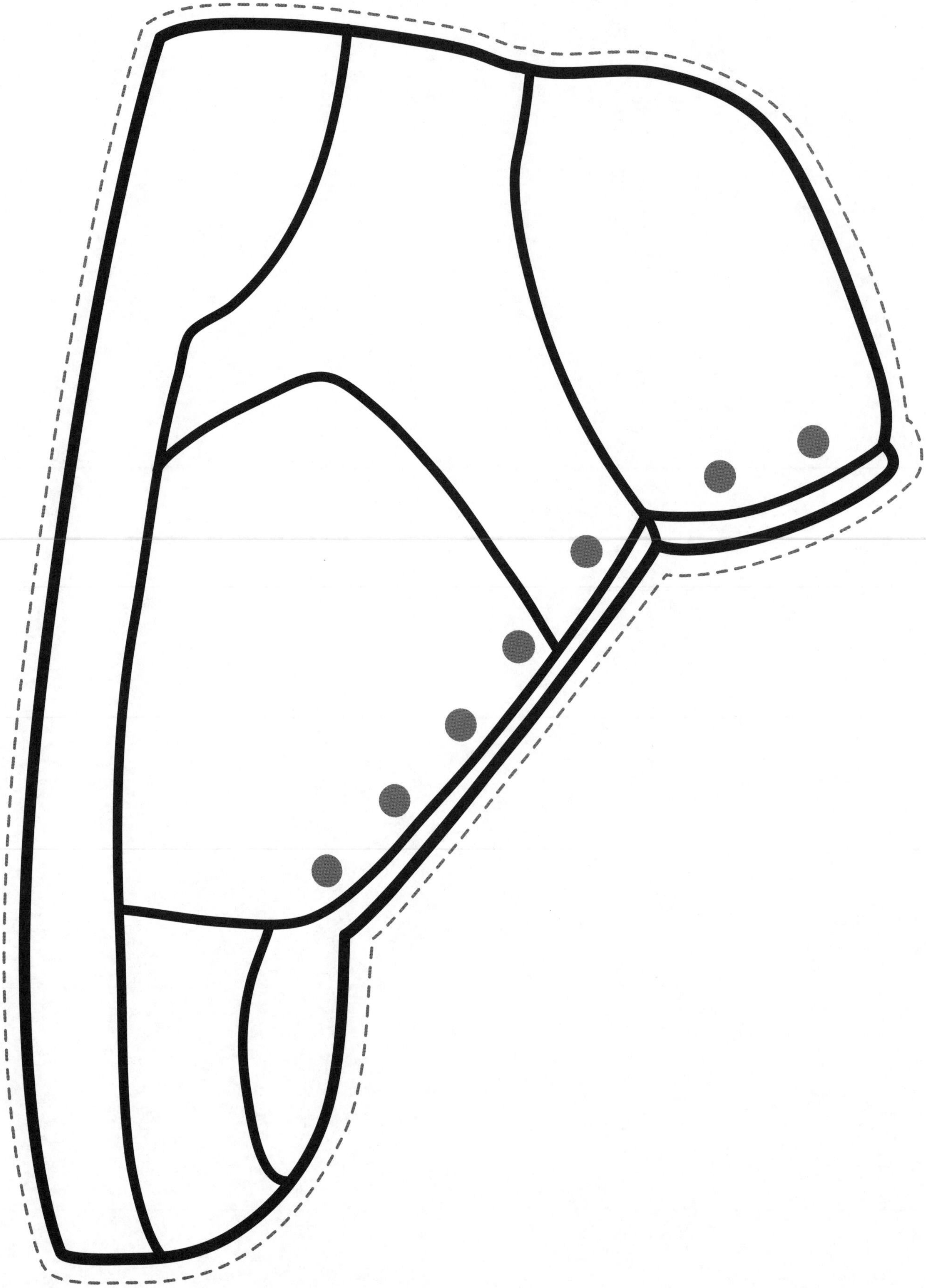

Children Need Shoes

Skills:
Subtract;
Solve word problems;
Add;
Count;
Use visual information

Over 300 million children around the world do not own a pair of shoes.

Answer the items.

1. Gate Elementary has 143 students. But only 87 students own a pair of shoes. How many students do **not** own a pair of shoes?

   _____ students do not own a pair of shoes.

   Show Your Work

2. Every student at school needs a pair of shoes. Ms. Zuri's class has 21 students. Mr. Joe's class has 34 students. Mrs. Baku's class has 27 students. How many students need shoes?

   _____ students need shoes.

   Show Your Work

Look at the picture. Then answer the items.

3. How many children? _____

   How many feet on each child? _____

   How many feet in all? _____

Skills:
Recognize functions of shoes;
Make inferences to match shoe descriptions to people's needs;
Formulate a creative idea for shoe technology

Shoes That Help

Engineers have used technology in shoes to help people in many ways. Some shoes have gel on the bottom to protect people's heels and keep them comfortable.

Read. Then match the people to the kind of shoe they need.

Who Needs the Help	Technology That Helps
Children who cannot buy new shoes. •	• Shoes that can track the number of steps you take.
People who want to stay healthy. •	• Shoes that can heat up your feet.
People who live in cold weather. •	• Shoes that can grow up to 5 sizes larger.

If you could design a new kind of shoe, what would it be able to do? How would it help people?

____

____

Shoe Designer

Shoe designers are people who make and design shoes. They design shoes to help people in many ways.

Skills:
Use visual information and context clues to make inferences;
Learn how shoe designers can help people;
Formulate and justify an opinion

Read. Then choose a shoe that is best for the person.

boots

sandals

ballet shoes

Hi, my name is Hector. I love to go to the beach. I need a shoe that is good to wear in hot weather. I also need a shoe that will make it easy to dump out all the sand that I pick up from the beach. Which shoe do I need?

Hector should wear the ______________________________ because

____.

Skills:
Problem solving;
Creative skills;
Solving problem-based, authentic tasks;
Multiple methods;
Multiple content areas;
Connected ideas;
Technology integration

Problem to Solve

Your school is collecting pairs of shoes to give away to other children who do not have shoes. You will give away old shoes. Decorate an old pair of shoes to make them look new.

Task

First, do the research on the next page. Then brainstorm and design on page 32. Last, decorate your shoes.

Rule

- Use an old pair of shoes to decorate. Or if you do not have an old pair of shoes, make a pair of shoes from materials in your home.

Things you might use

Painted Shoes

Skills:
Conduct research;
Make observations;
Use visual information;
Hypothesize;
Answer questions based on research

Read. Look at the picture. Then answer the items.

1. What was used to redesign these shoes?

____

2. Do you like these shoes? Tell why or why not.

____

____

3. What will make children want to wear these shoes?

____

____

Problem & Task → Research → **Brainstorm & Design** → Make It & Explain It

Skills:
Use concepts to solve a non-routine problem;
Apply concepts;
Design a way to decorate old shoes;
Create a solution to a problem;
Explain a design;
Brainstorm ideas to repair shoes

New Shoes Brainstorm

Answer the items to help you brainstorm ideas for your shoe design.

1. What can you use to cover a hole in a shoe?

____

2. What are some things around the house you could use to make your shoes more soft or comfortable to wear?

____

3. What will make children want to wear your shoes?

____

Now draw a picture of what your shoes will look like. Think about what you will use.

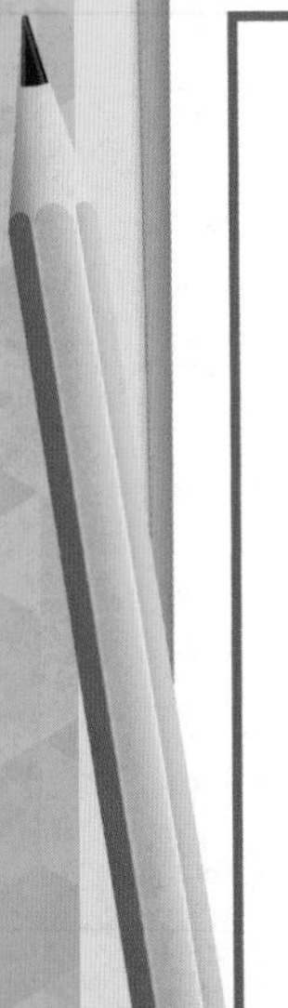

My New Shoes

Decorate your old shoes or make the shoes that you drew.

Then take a picture of them and glue it below.
Or draw a picture of your finished work in the box.

Finish the sentences to tell more about what you made.

I used ______________________________ to make these shoes look new. I think children will like them because

____

____

____.

Skills:

Create original decorations for old shoes;

Explain the purpose of the design;

Draw or present visual information;

Evaluate a design

Concepts:

Some people who live in senior living communities have a difficult time adjusting and miss their loved ones who do not live with them;

There are facilities that provide care to seniors who need more help than their families can give them;

As people get older, their bodies and abilities change;

It can be difficult for people to see their older loved ones move to a senior living facility

Read the story. Think about the problems in the story.

Cheering Up Grandpa

Jane was worried about her grandpa. He fell again this morning, and she didn't know if he went to the hospital or not. "Grandpa, I'm home!" yelled Jane after school. She went straight into his bedroom, but he wasn't there. She found her mom in the garage loading boxes into the car. "Mom, is Grandpa at the hospital again?"

"No, honey," said Jane's mom. "Grandpa is at the senior care center. He's going to live there now."

"What! Why?" asked Jane. "What about our music?" Jane and Grandpa played guitar and sang songs most days.

"I'm sorry, honey, but he needs more care than what we can give him here. He hurt his arm when he fell, and now he cannot even use his walker." Jane hugged her mom tightly.

Jane called her grandpa every week. He sounded sad when she talked to him. This made Jane feel sad. One Saturday, Jane's parents drove her to visit Grandpa. When Jane got there, she took out her guitar and sang her grandpa's favorite songs. He smiled and sang along with her. He looked happier already.

Cheer Up

Helping Grandpa

Answer the items about the story you read.

1. Draw a picture of one problem you read about in the story. Then write a sentence about it.

One problem in the story is ______________________________

____.

2. How was the problem fixed?

This problem was fixed when ______________________________

____.

3. If your grandpa were sad, how would you cheer him up?

I would ____

____.

Skills:

Identify key problems and ideas in a text;

Summarize a problem;

Formulate a solution to a problem;

Produce a creative drawing to interpret a problem

Cheer Up

Feeling Lonely

Being around others can make people happy. The friendships we share help us live, grow, and be the best we can be. But as a person gets older, he or she might spend less time with others. Sometimes, it is because the older person does not live near loved ones. Sometimes, it is because older people cannot get around as easily. So it is harder for them to visit their friends and family. This can make the older people, like our grandparents, feel sad and lonely.

Being Alone Can Change Your Body

Some scientists believe that our health gets better when we spend time with others. Talking with people can help your thinking skills. Talking with others helps your mind grow stronger. But our health can change when we spend less time being social. People can get sad when they have nobody to talk to or play with. When people are sad, they do not feel like exercising or going on walks. Getting exercise is important to stay healthy and not get sick. So having a friend around not only makes you happier, but it can help you stay healthy, too.

Concepts:
Social interaction is important for our health;
There are things we can do to bring joy to people in senior living facilities who feel sad

What You Can Do

Doing acts of kindness for older people can make them feel happier and less lonely. Here are some things you can do with your grandparents or older people in your community:

- Take a walk together in nature.
- Play a board game together.
- Do art projects together.
- Read your favorite books aloud to them.
- Sing or dance for them.
- Talk with them often, and let them know how special they are to you.

Skills:

Convey an idea through visual art;

Explore uses of materials and tools to create works of art or design;

Demonstrate creativity

Picture Book

Picture books with positive words can help cheer you up when you feel sad.

Make a picture book for your older loved ones to cheer them up.

What You Need

- cutouts on page 39
- 3 sheets of paper
- colored pencils or markers
- stapler
- glue

What You Do

1. First, stack 3 sheets of paper together and fold them in half.
2. Then staple the pages together along the side that is folded.
3. Next, cut out the positive words on page 39 and glue one on each page of your book. Then draw pictures on each page.
4. Last, decorate the front cover of your book and give it to an older person in your life.

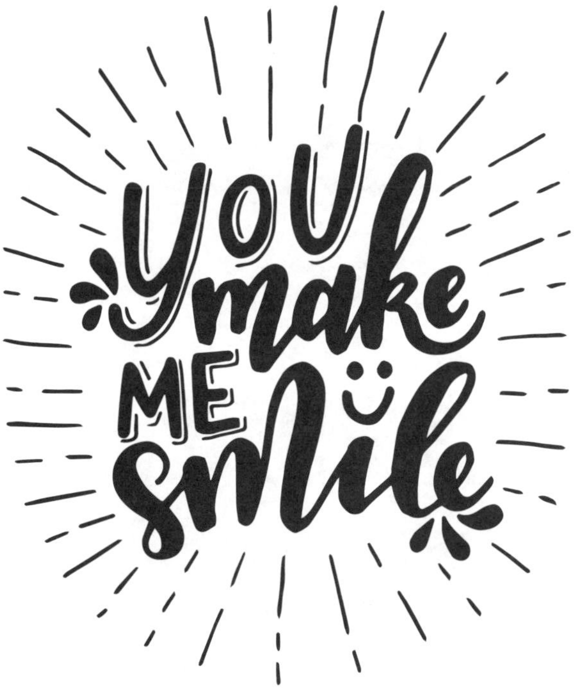
You make me smile

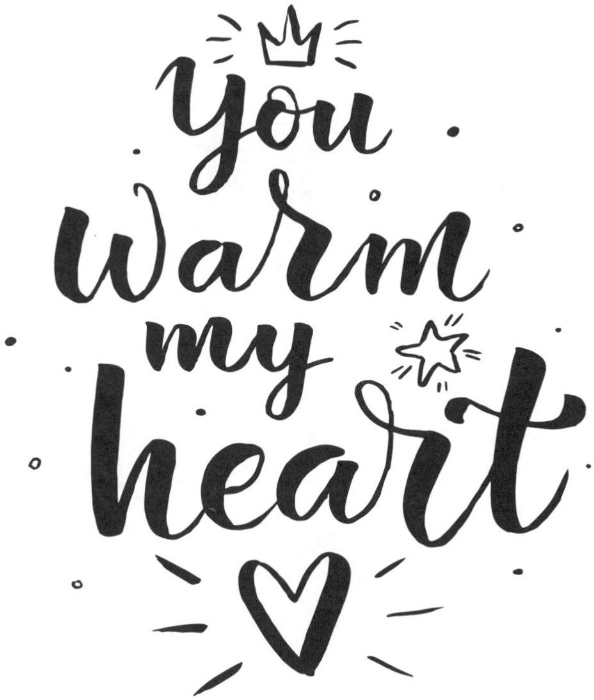
You warm my heart

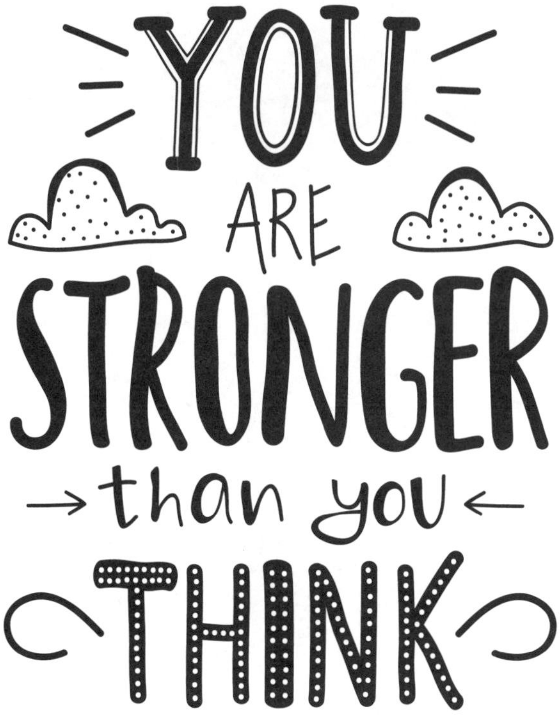
YOU ARE STRONGER than you THINK

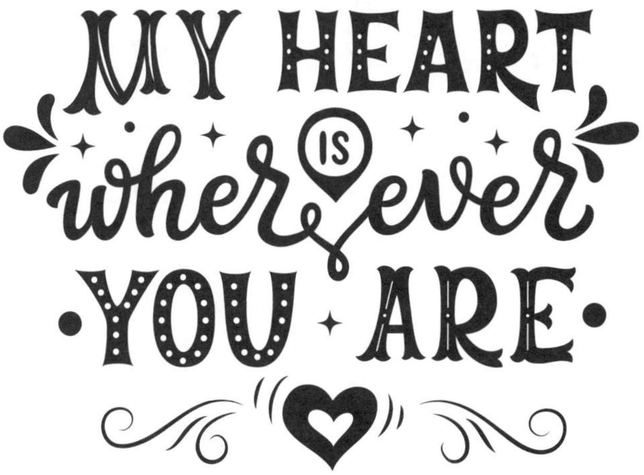
MY HEART IS wherever YOU ARE

Music Memory

Skills:
Identify words that rhyme;
Learn about memory-enhancing strategies;
Create a rhyming phrase

We sometimes forget things as we get older. Our memories can change over time. Music and rhyming words can help people remember things.

Fill in the circle to choose a word that rhymes.

1. Play, dance, hop, or **run**,
exercise can be lots of ___.

Ⓐ work Ⓑ fun

2. If your days don't seem so **bright**,
I'll be there to shine a ___.

Ⓐ beam Ⓑ light

3. Read a love **letter**,
To make you smile and feel ___.

Ⓐ better Ⓑ good

Make a rhyme using the words **frown** and **down**.

4. ______________________________

____

Skills:

Recognize devices and their definitions;

Use clues to match devices and their functions

Keep in Touch

Technology helps people stay in touch with each other.

Read the clues. Use the words in the box to solve the puzzle.

hearing aid	letter	car
computer	wheelchair	phone

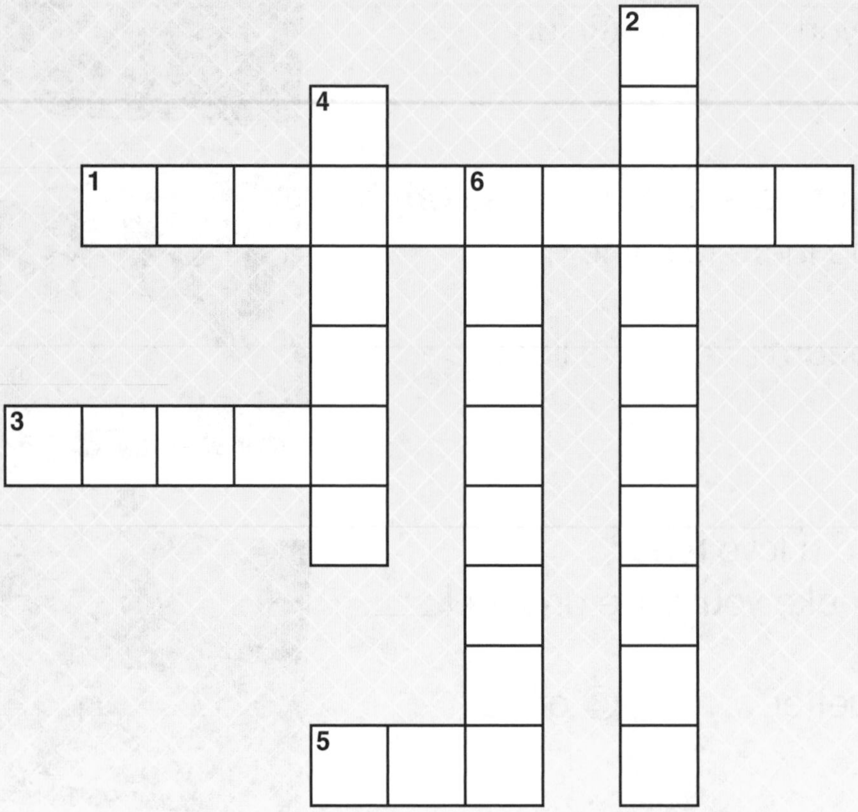

Across

1. This helps people who have trouble walking.
3. You use this to call people.
5. You use this to drive places.

Down

2. This helps people hear.
4. This is something you send in the mail.
6. You use this to contact people on the Internet.

Community Center Leader

A community center leader is a person who plans fun events for members of their community.

Skills:
Apply information to produce creative writing;
Learn about a career that helps people connect

The community center leader needs your help! Grandparents' Day is coming up, and the center needs a fun activity for kids to do with their grandparents. Pick an activity like painting, dancing, or decorating a cake. Then make a flyer in the box to tell others about it.

Skills:
Problem solving;
Creative skills;
Solving problem-based, authentic tasks;
Multiple methods;
Multiple content areas;
Connected ideas;
Technology integration

Problem to Solve

Some of the seniors at the Happy Elder Care Center need to be cheered up. They feel sad because they miss their families and old friends. You will write a song and make a dance to perform for the people at Happy Elder Care Center.

Task

First, do research on the next page. Then brainstorm and design on page 46. Last, write your song on page 47 and make a dance to perform.

Rules

- The song must have 4 or more words that rhyme.
- You must do two or more different moves in your dance, such as jump and clap.

Things you might use

Songs to Make You Dance

Sing the song. Look at the pictures.
Then answer the items.

If you're feeling sad and blue,
I know what you need to do!
Swing your arms and stomp your feet,
It's fun to dance to the beat!

1. Does the song rhyme? If so, write the words below.

____________________ rhymes with ____________________.

____________________ rhymes with ____________________.

2. Do you see dance moves you would like to do?

Ⓐ yes   Ⓑ no

Skills:
Conduct research;
Use visual information;
Make observations;
Answer items based on a text;
Plan

Problem & Task → Research → **Brainstorm & Design** → Make It & Explain It

Skills:

Use concepts to solve a non-routine problem;

Apply concepts;

Brainstorm song lyrics that rhyme;

Create a solution to a problem;

Design dance moves

Song Brainstorm

Answer the items to help you brainstorm ideas for a song.

1. Songs can be about many different things. Some songs are about our favorite foods. Some songs are about the things we like to do. Write down some things you would like to sing about.

   For example, you might sing about how much you love your pets.

   ____

   ____

2. Write words that rhyme that you might want to use in your song.

   ______________ rhymes with ______________.

   ______________ rhymes with ______________.

3. Do you have a favorite song? If so, write the name of the song below.

   ____

4. Now listen to the song, and make up your own words to the tune. Do your favorite dance moves, too!

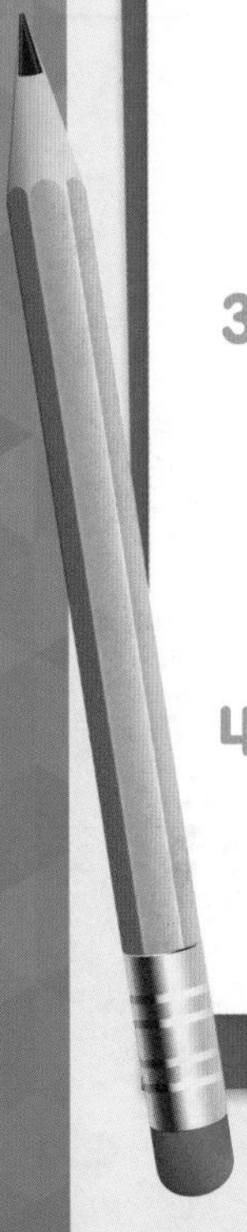

My Happy Song and Dance

Write your song below. Dance to and sing your song for a grandparent or friend. Then draw a picture of you doing your favorite dance moves.

My song is called ______________________________.

This is how it goes:

____

____

____

______________________________.

Skills:

Draw to convey an original idea;

Create dance moves;

Write a song;

Draw or present visual information;

Use creativity

Concepts:

Some families cannot afford school supplies;

Some schools do not have enough supplies for every student;

Insufficient supplies can affect a student's learning

Read the story. Think about the problems in the story.

Not Enough Supplies

"Class, we are going to paint pictures now," said Mrs. Yang. "We have only two paintbrushes, though, so we have to take turns. Carl and Joanne, you will go first. The rest of you will practice writing words until it's your turn. Now take out your paper and pencils and start working."

Lance took out paper. But he did not have a pencil. He lost his and his mom did not have enough money to buy him more. "Mrs. Yang, I need a pencil," he said.

"Sorry, Lance, I don't have a pencil for you," said Mrs. Lang. "Just sit and wait for your turn to paint." Lance shrugged. He could not do his work and he felt bored. He waited for what felt like a long time. Then Lupin said, "Hey, Lance, you can use my pencil while I paint." Lance thanked Lupin and started writing. A little while later, it was Lance's turn to paint.

He had only been painting for a short time when the teacher rang a bell. "It's time to clean up and go home!" she said. "But I'm not finished!" said Lance. "It's not fair. We didn't have enough paintbrushes or enough time!"

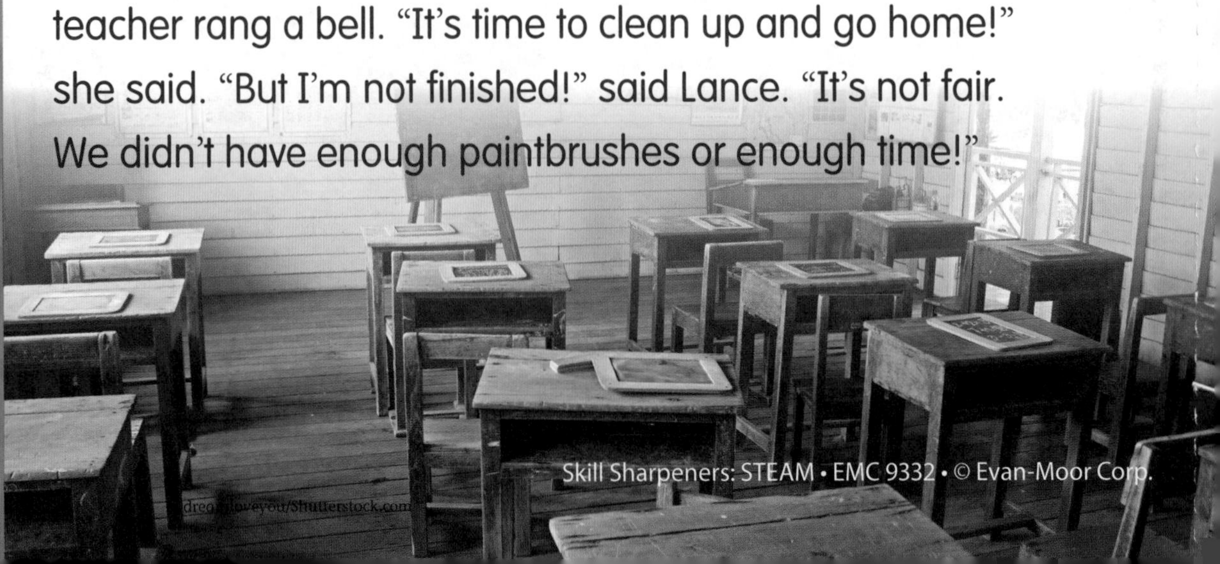

…loveyou/Shutterstock.com

Lance's Problems

Skills:
Identify key problems and ideas in a text;
Summarize a problem;
Formulate an opinion;
Produce a creative drawing to interpret a problem

Answer the items about the story you read.

1. Draw a picture of one problem you read about in the story. Then write a sentence about it.

One problem in the story is ______________________________

____.

2. Why couldn't Lance finish his painting?

He could not finish because ______________________________

____.

3. Do you think classrooms need to have enough art and school supplies? Why or why not?

____

____

Schools Need Supplies

What does your classroom look like? Does it have clean floors, a whiteboard or a chalkboard, and tables and chairs for all students? Are there books, pencils, and paper for you to use?

Classrooms Around the World

Many schools do not have the things students need to learn. Some schools do not have money to build classrooms.

© Dietmar Temps / Shutterstock.com

They learn outside. And some schools do not have a lot of space. Classrooms can have 60 or more students in one room. That's a lot of students!

© Dietmar Temps / Shutterstock.com

© Cheboite Titus / Shutterstock.com

Concepts:
Some schools lack basic supplies to help their students learn;
Some classrooms have a high number of students for every teacher, which can make learning more difficult

© JLwarehouse / Shutterstock.com

Some schools have many classrooms, but their supplies are very old.

Supplies Needed

Students need basic school supplies such as paper, pencils, and books to do their work. If students do not have the supplies they need, it makes it hard to learn. When students do not have supplies, they sometimes do not go to school.

Many schools around the world need supplies like these:

- tables and chairs
- pencils and paper
- books
- chalkboards or whiteboards
- art supplies like paint and colored pencils
- scissors and glue
- computers

Skills:

Convey an idea through visual art;

Explore uses of materials and tools to create works of art or design;

Use observation and investigation in preparation for making a work of art;

Demonstrate creativity

Fundraiser Flyer

People or groups try to help schools get what they need by fundraising, or asking people or businesses to give money to schools. Fundraisers often make flyers or posters that explain what the schools need and why.

Make a flyer that explains why you need people's help to raise money for schools to buy supplies.

Step 1: Brainstorm

- What are some common supplies schools need?
- Why do schools need supplies?
- How can people help schools get more supplies?
- How can you decorate your flyer to get people to notice it and give money?

Step 2: Do Research

Think about these questions as you look at the flyer:

- Does this flyer catch your eye?
- Who needs help?
- Why do they need help?
- What do they need?
- How can people help with the problem?

Step 3: Plan

Choose the things you want to use.
Things you might use:

Draw what you would like to put on your flyer.
Think about the supplies schools need.

Step 4: Make It and Share It

Make your flyer. Then show it to a friend and tell them why you made it.

Coins for School Supplies

Skills:
Add and subtract;
Solve word problems;
Use addition and subtraction strategies

Many schools around the world do not have money to buy the supplies students need to learn.

Answer the items.

1. The books your school needs cost 200 coins. But your school only has 65 coins. How many more coins does your school need to buy the books?

   65 + ______ = 200

Show Your Work

2. Your class is selling cupcakes to earn money for books. Each cupcake costs 20 coins. If you sold 3 cupcakes, how many coins did you earn?

Show Your Work

_____ + _____ + _____ = _____ coins

Skills:

Use visual information to compare and contrast forms of technology;

Use visual information to match older and newer forms of technology;

Recognize that schools need supplies

School Supplies

Classroom Technology

A technology tool helps us do work. Some schools have new technology tools, such as TVs and computers. But many schools do not even have simple technology tools, such as pencils and paper.

Match the old technology to the new technology.

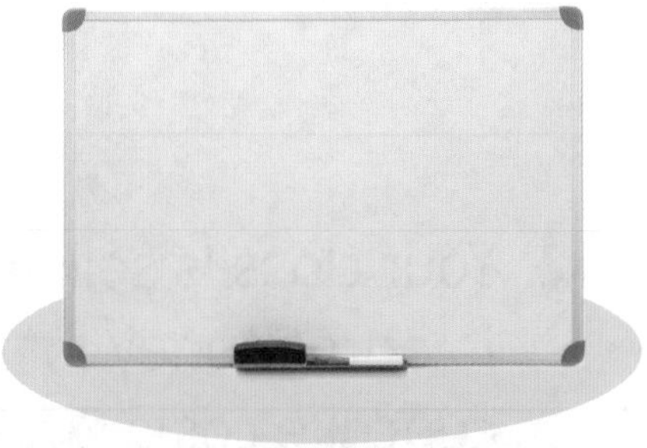

Fundraising Jobs

Some people's jobs are to raise money to help others.

Read about the people. Then read the job descriptions. Write the name to match a person to a job.

Skills:
Use visual information and informational text to make inferences;
Learn about careers that help raise money for good causes

Volunteers

Edith
I like to plan parties. I am fun, friendly, and creative.

Vinny
I love meeting new people. I am good at making art and using technology.

Jason
I am great at math.

Jobs

Money Counter

- keeps track of all money
- uses money to buy supplies

____

Event Planner

- plans fun events to raise money
- must be friendly and creative

____

Community Worker

- makes videos and flyers
- finds other people to help, too

____

STEAM Task

Problem & Task → Research → Brainstorm & Design → Make It & Explain It

Skills:
Problem solving;
Creative skills;
Solving problem-based, authentic tasks;
Multiple methods;
Multiple content areas;
Connected ideas;
Technology integration

School Supplies

Problem to Solve

Some families do not have enough money to buy backpacks or school supplies. Your class wants to fill backpacks with school supplies and give them to students who need them. But you need money to buy the supplies. You will make a video to tell people about this problem and ask them to give, or donate, money for backpacks and school supplies.

Task

First, do research on the next page. Then brainstorm and plan on page 60 what you will say in your video. Next, record the video. Last, draw a picture on page 61.

Rule

- In the video, tell these things:
  - ✓ who you want to help
  - ✓ how you are going to help
  - ✓ how others can help

Things you might use

Video for Shoes

This student made a video to raise money and help children who need shoes. Read what he said in the video. Then answer the items.

1. Who needs help?

____

2. Why do they need help?

____

3. How is this boy helping?

____

4. How can others help, too?

____

Skills:

Conduct research;

Make observations;

Use visual information;

Hypothesize;

Answer questions based on research

Skills:
Use concepts to solve a non-routine problem;
Apply concepts;
Design a video presentation;
Create a solution to a problem;
Explain a design

Problem & Task → Research → **Brainstorm & Design** → Make It & Explain It

Brainstorm Video Ideas

Answer the items to help you brainstorm ideas for your video.

1. Do all schools have supplies to help students learn?

   Ⓐ yes Ⓑ no

2. Why do students need supplies?

   ____

3. How are you going to help?

   ____

4. Write a list of supplies you will put into the backpacks for students.

   ______________ ______________

   ______________ ______________

   ______________ ______________

5. How can people who see your video help, too?

   ____

   ____

School Supplies

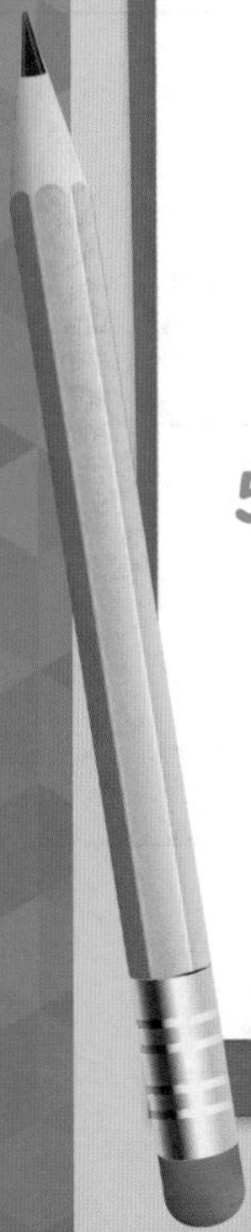

Record the Video

Write what you would like to say in your video. Then record your video, and say everything you want to say.

Last, draw a picture that shows you helping.

____

____

____

____

____

Skills:

Create an informative video presentation;

Write a script for a video presentation

Draw or present visual information;

Evaluate a design;

Practice self-awareness

Concepts:
Animals need proper care to be healthy;
Some people depend on animals to help do work

Read the story. Think about the problems in the story.

Farming on the Mountain

Andrea looked down from her farm high up in the mountains. She could see the market at the bottom of the hill where her family sold the tomatoes they grew. Andrea fed her donkey, wrapped up ripe tomatoes, and put them into bags. Then she loaded the heavy bags onto her donkey and began to slowly walk down the long, rocky mountain trail. The donkey would carry the bags all the way to the market.

Halfway down the hill, the donkey started to slow down. Then it made a loud “Hee-haw” and laid on the ground. It would not move. “What’s wrong, Donkey?” asked Andrea. “Are the bags too heavy?” Andrea took off some bags, and the donkey stood up. It was ready to walk now, and they continued down the mountain.

The hot sun beat down on them. Suddenly, the donkey slowed down and walked over to stand in the shade of a small tree. “What’s wrong now, Donkey?” asked Andrea. The donkey looked hot and tired, so Andrea gave it some water and let it rest. After a few minutes, it was ready to move again. Andrea knew from that day on she had to take better care of her donkey if it was going to help her get to the market.

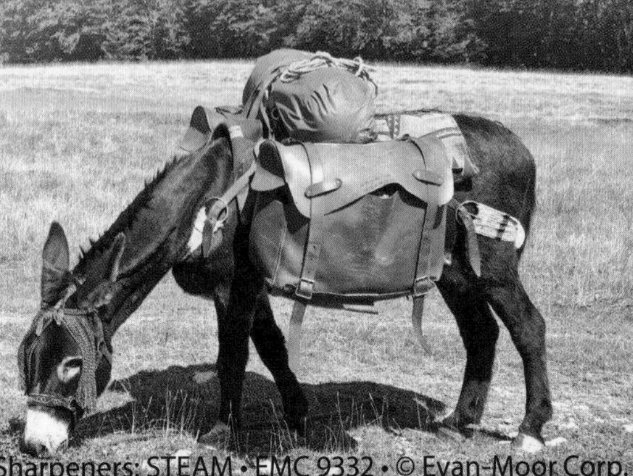

Taking Care of Animals

Answer the items about the story you read.

1. Draw a picture of one problem you read about in the story. Then write a sentence about it.

One problem in the story is ______________________________

____.

2. How was the problem fixed?

This problem was fixed when ___________________________

____.

3. Why do you think it is important for Andrea to keep her donkey healthy?

It is important because _______________________________

____.

Skills:
Identify key problems and ideas in a text;
Summarize a problem;
Demonstrate understanding of a text;
Produce a creative drawing to interpret a problem

Working Animals

Working Animals

People in some places use technology to help them do work. Tractors or machines help farmers plant and harvest crops. Big trucks help move heavy loads from place to place. But some people around the world do not have much technology to help them. These people depend on animals to help them do work. But animals sometimes get sick or hurt while working.

How Animals Help

For many years, people have used animals to help them do work. Pack animals help by carrying people, crops, and goods on their backs. Pack animals are often used in places where it is too hard to drive a car or other vehicle. Farmers that live high up in the mountains strap heavy bags or baskets filled with crops onto the backs of donkeys. The donkeys travel down the steep, rocky trails so farmers can sell their goods to the markets. Other pack animals include horses, llamas, and camels.

How Work Hurts

Animals that work sometimes get sick or hurt. Some animals work many hours and do not get a chance to rest. Carrying or pulling a load that is too heavy can hurt an animal. Sometimes, the saddles people use to ride animals can hurt the animals, too. Some animals do work in places with rough land, like on the trails of the mountain. Working on rough terrain for many hours can cause scrapes or cuts on the hooves, or feet, of an animal.

How to Help

© GEORGE STAMATIS / Shutterstock.com

Animals that are happy and healthy are able to work. Animals need food, water, and rest to stay healthy. If an ox is tired, it may take a long time to do work. But if the ox is well-rested and well-fed, it will have the strength and energy to do the work faster. All working animals deserve respect, rest, food, and water to stay healthy.

Concepts:
Animals need proper care;
Some people depend on working animals to survive;
There are many different kinds of working animals

Skills:

Convey an idea through visual art;

Explore uses of materials and tools to create works of art or design;

Use observation and investigation in preparation for making a work of art;

Demonstrate creativity

Llama Tassels

In Peru, llamas are used to carry crops and goods on their backs. Some people decorate their llamas with colorful tassels to help them know which llamas belong to them. Tassels also tell if the llama is a boy or a girl.

Now it's your turn to make a necklace for your llama.

What You Need

- different colored yarn
- scissors
- 10-inch piece of cardboard
- string
- rubber bands
- directions on pages 67 and 68

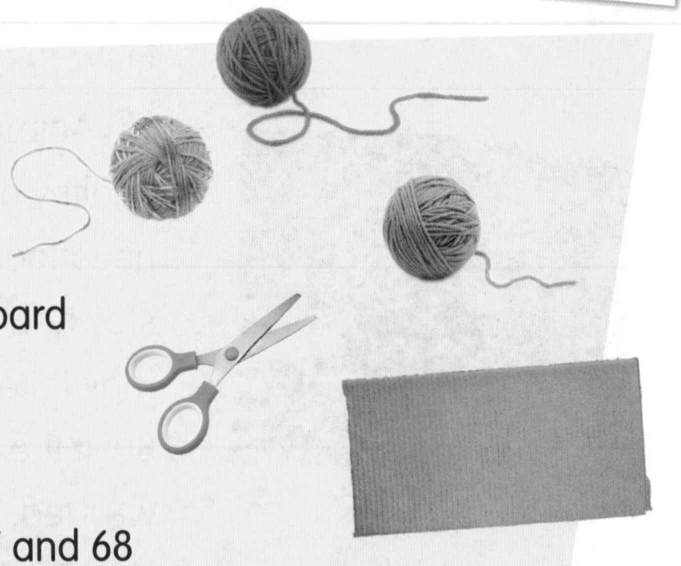

What You Do

1. First, wrap the yarn around the piece of cardboard many times.

2. Then slide the yarn off the cardboard and lay it flat.

3. Next, cut the loops of yarn at both ends. You should have one big pile of yarn.

4. Take one piece of yarn from the pile and tie it tightly around the yarn a couple times.

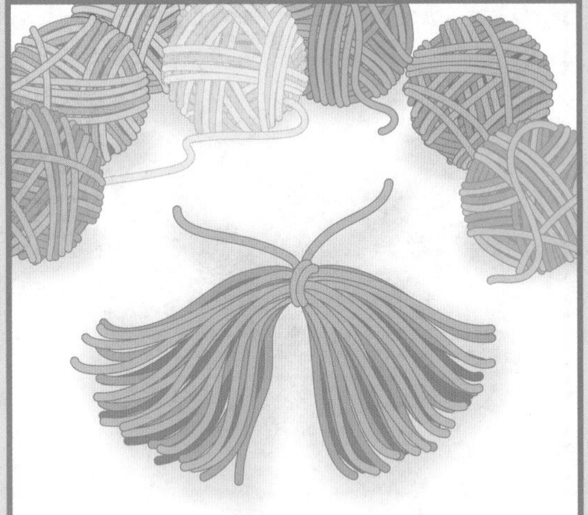

5. It should now look like this.

6. Pinch the yarn together and wrap a rubber band around it. Repeat steps 1–6 to make more tassels.

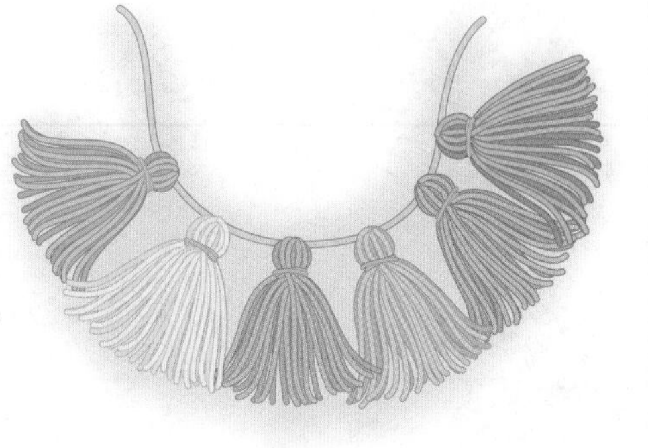

7. Then cut a long piece of string. Tie the tassels along the string.

8. Finally, connect the ends of the string to finish your necklace.

Heavy Loads

Skills:
Compare numbers;
Use context to match;
Demonstrate understanding of weight

Animals are strong and can carry a lot of weight on their backs. But loads that are too heavy can hurt animals. It is important to know how much weight each pack animal can hold. Camels are very strong and can carry a very heavy load. A horse cannot carry more weight than a camel. A donkey cannot carry more weight than a horse.

Match the animal to how much weight it can carry on its back.

300 pounds

125 pounds

600 pounds

Skills:

Use visual information;

Learn about alternative forms of technology and energy;

Recognize how working animals can help people do work

Animals and Technology

People use animals and technology to help them do work. Some farmers have oxen pull plows to loosen the soil on their farms. Some people use horses to pull them in wagons.

Look at the pictures. Then unscramble the word to tell which piece of technology is being used in each picture.

1. D E L S

____ ____ ____ ____

2. L W O P

____ ____ ____ ____

3. G N W A O

____ ____ ____ ____ ____

Veterinarian

A veterinarian is an animal doctor. A vet helps sick or hurt animals. A vet can tell you how to keep your pet animals happy and healthy.

Skills:
Use visual information and informational text to form an answer;
Learn about veterinarians

Look at the picture. Read the paragraph and all of the sentences below. Then draw an **X** in the box if the sentence tells a way to help the horse be healthy.

This horse is having trouble carrying heavy loads. The horse walks very slowly and has no energy. The bottom of the horse's hooves are worn down.

- ☐ Braid the horse's hair.
- ☐ Feed the horse healthy meals.
- ☐ Give the horse horseshoes to protect its worn hooves.
- ☐ Make the horse work harder.
- ☐ Give the horse smaller loads to carry.

Skills:
Problem solving;
Creative skills;
Solving problem-based, authentic tasks;
Multiple methods;
Multiple content areas;
Connected ideas;
Technology integration

Problem to Solve

The people in a village have animals that help do work. But the animals are getting hurt and feeling sick. The people do not know how to take good care of the animals. Your job is to make a handbook that teaches people how to take care of their working animals.

Task

First, do research on the next page. Then brainstorm and plan the book on page 74. Next, make your book. Last, answer the item on page 75.

Rules

- The book must have a picture of the 2 working animals you will read about on page 73.
- The book must tell what each animal needs to stay healthy.
- The book must tell why it is important for the animals to be healthy.

Things you might use

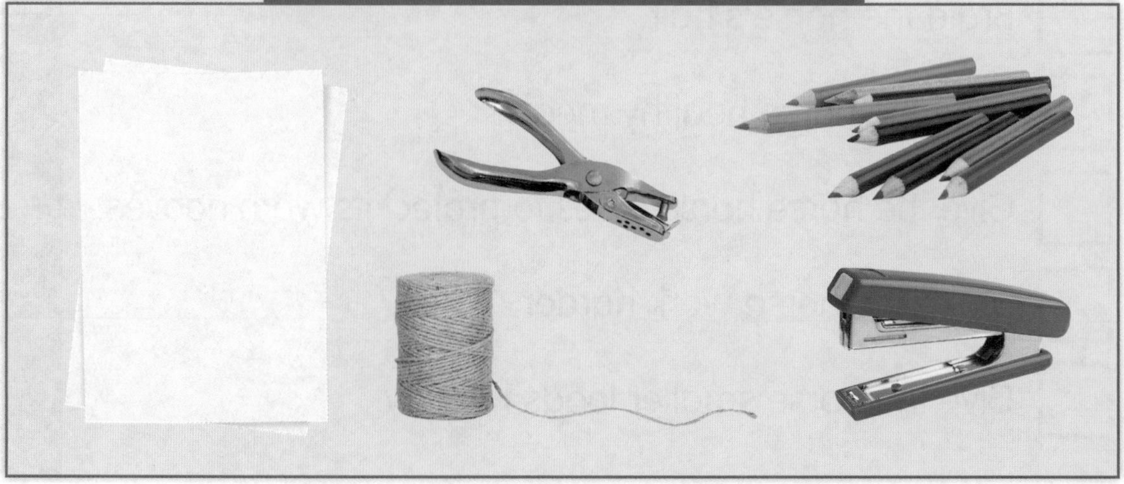

Animals That Help

Look at the pictures.
Read about the animals.

Donkeys

- Donkeys should be fed hay, grass, and other small plants during the day.
- Carrots, apples, turnips, and pears are sweet treats for donkeys.
- Donkeys need clean water to drink.
- Donkeys need rest and shelter.

Sled Dogs

© tipwam / Shutterstock.com

- Sled dogs need healthy meals to give them energy to pull sleds. Dogs must eat at least once a day.
- Some people feed dogs meat and rice. Dogs can also eat dry dog food and kibble.
- Dogs need clean water, plenty of rest, and shelter.
- Most sled dogs need to play with other dogs to stay happy.
- The nails on the dogs' paws should be cut sometimes to keep the dogs from getting hurt.

Skills:
Conduct research;
Make observations;
Use visual information;
Hypothesize;
Answer questions based on research

Problem & Task → Research → **Brainstorm & Design** → Make It & Explain It

Handbook Brainstorm

Answer the items to help you brainstorm ideas for your handbook.

Skills:
Use concepts to solve a non-routine problem;
Apply concepts;
Design and plan a handbook;
Create a solution to a problem;
Explain a design

1. What are some ways animals get hurt or sick?

____

____

2. Why is it important to keep all animals healthy?

____

____

3. What can people do to help animals stay safe and healthy?

____

____

4. What will you use to make your handbook?

____

____

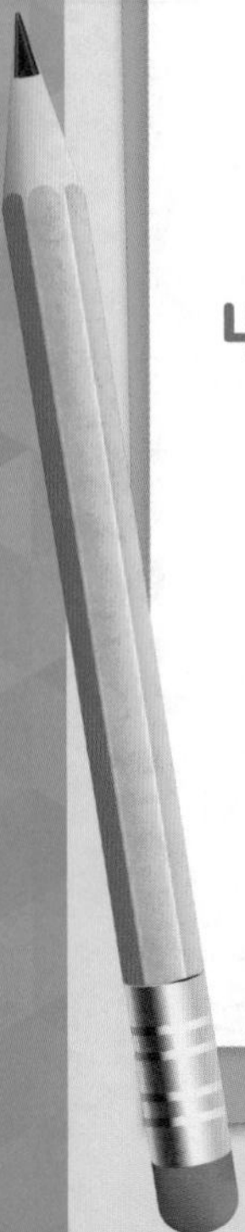

Working Animal Handbook

Make your handbook.

Then draw a picture of the animals you wrote about in the box below. Last, finish the sentences to tell more about your handbook.

I wrote this handbook to help people take good care

of working animals. This handbook tells what

_______________ and _______________ need to stay healthy.

Skills:

Construct a handbook;

Explain the function of the handbook;

Draw or present visual information;

Evaluate a design

Concepts:
Sometimes people who bully others feel bad and want to change;
Sometimes people do not know they are bullying others;
Bullying can make people feel sad;
It can be difficult to be different or feel different from other people

Bullying

Read the story. Think about the problems in the story.

Do Not Be a Bully

Jesse loves to go to school. But he does not learn as quickly as the other children. Reading is hard for Jesse, but he always tries his best.

One day, Jesse's teacher asked him to read out loud to the class. Jesse read the sentence, "I see the **is-land**."

"Close, Jesse. Say that last word again," said the teacher. Jesse tried again,"**Iss-land**."

"HA-HA! He said it wrong, AGAIN! It is **eye-land**. He is such a dummy!" said Jesse's classmate Timmy. The whole class laughed. This made Jesse very sad. Jesse's friend Alison stood up from her desk. She looked at Timmy and said, "Hey, do not be a bully! That was not a nice thing to say!"

Timmy looked over at Jesse and saw that he was sad. Timmy feels sad, too, when his older brothers tease him. Timmy felt bad about making Jesse sad. "Teasing hurts people. I'll try to be nicer to my classmates," Timmy thought to himself.

Class Bully

Skills:
Identify key problems and ideas in a text;
Summarize a problem;
Empathize with a character in a story;
Produce a creative drawing to interpret a problem

Answer the items about the story you read.

1. Draw a picture of one problem you read about in the story. Then write a sentence about it.

One problem in the story is ______________________________

______________________________.

2. How would you feel if you were Jesse?

I would feel ______________________________

______________________________.

3. What would you do if someone was bullying you?

I would ______________________________

______________________________.

Be a Friend, Not a Bully

It is important to treat people the way that you want to be treated. But not everyone follows this rule. A bully is a person who hurts people on purpose. A bully often hurts the same person many times. Sometimes, the person getting hurt does not know how to make the bully stop.

Being a Bully

A bully can be a boy or a girl who does things or says things to hurt others.

A bully can hurt others by

- yelling or saying mean things,
- pushing or hitting others, or
- not letting others play.

Bullies sometimes hurt people because they feel sad or angry. They do not know how to deal with their feelings. Some bullies think being mean makes them look cool. But bullying is never cool.

Being Bullied

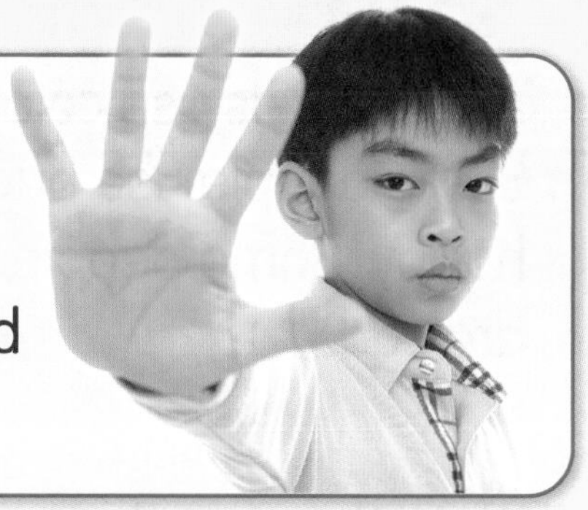

If you are being bullied,

- tell the bully to STOP,
- walk away and talk to an adult, and
- stay near other kids or adults.

If someone is hurting you, do not keep it a secret. Share your feelings with someone you trust, like a parent or a teacher. They can help stop the bullying.

Stand Up to Bullies

Sometimes, the people being bullied need help. Always tell an adult if you see someone being bullied. You can also help by being kind to the person being bullied and listen to how they feel.

You can show respect for yourself and other people by being mindful. Being mindful means to think about how you feel and how your body feels. Being mindful can help you stay calm if you are bullied or feel like you want to bully someone.

Concepts:
It is important to safely stand up to bullying;
Sometimes people who do bullying just need some help learning how to act when they have certain feelings;
Everyone deserves to be treated with respect

Bullying

Skills:

Convey an idea through visual art;

Explore uses of materials and tools to create works of art or design;

Use observation and investigation in preparation for making a work of art;

Demonstrate creativity

Colors and Feelings

Many artists use colors in their art to show how they feel. Some people use bright colors to show when they are happy. Some people use dark colors to show when they are sad.

Follow the steps below.

What You Need

- coloring page and cutouts on page 81
- markers or colored pencils
- glue or tape
- scissors
- pencil

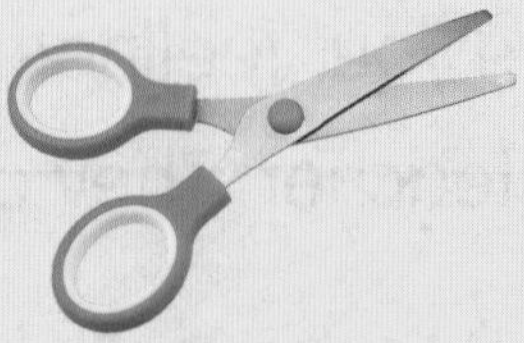

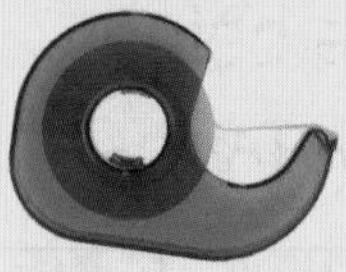

What You Do

1. Choose a feeling picture on page 81 or draw your own in the circle. Then cut it out and glue it to finish the sentence on page 81.
2. Draw a picture on page 82 using colors that show how bullying makes you feel.

scared

sad

mad

Practice Mindfulness

Skills:
Learn about mindfulness;
Practice mindfulness activities

Your body and your mind work together to keep you healthy. Sometimes, you might not know what to do or say if you are mad or sad. You can practice being mindful. This is when you think about how you feel and why you feel that way.

Complete these steps to practice being mindful:

1. Sit on the floor.
2. Slowly take a big breath in through your nose.
3. Breathe out slowly through your mouth, like you are blowing out candles.
4. Now lie flat on your back on the floor.
5. Close your eyes.
6. Listen to the sounds around you.
7. Focus on any smells in the air.
8. Think about how the ground feels beneath you. Can you feel your heart beating? Are you sad, mad, or happy?

Skills:
Learn how different spaces can be used for different purposes;
Draw a design that meets a specific criteria and for a purpose

A Quiet Space

Some classrooms have a quiet place where students can go when they need to take a break. Students can read books, hold stuffed animals, or do puzzles or other quiet things. If you are feeling sad, mad, or tired, going to a quiet place can help you feel better.

Help your teacher design a quiet place in your classroom. Draw a picture of what it would look like. Then finish the sentence to tell more about it.

In the quiet place, you can ______________________________

____.

School Counselor

A school counselor is a person who students can talk to when they have a problem. A counselor can help students who are being bullied, having trouble learning, or having trouble making friends.

Skills:

Use visual information and informational text to choose answers;

Learn about the career of school counselors

Imagine that you are a school counselor. Fill in the circles that show how you can help when a bully hurts others.

○ 

Teach a student who is being bullied how to make the bully stop.

○ 

Join the bully and tease kids together.

○ 

Help the bully learn better ways to show feelings.

○ 

Talk and listen to both the bully and the other student's feelings.

Skills:
Problem solving;
Creative skills;
Solving problem-based, authentic tasks;
Multiple methods;
Multiple content areas;
Connected ideas;
Technology integration

Problem to Solve

Your friends are being bullied at school. But the bullies do not think they are doing anything wrong. The principal would like you to help. Write a play to show what bullying is and how to safely help stop bullying. Then have your friends or family act out the play.

Task

First, do the research on the next page. Then brainstorm and design on page 88. Last, write your play and answer the items on page 89.

Rules

- The play must have at least 3 characters.
- The play must show how a bully can hurt others.
- The play must show safe ways to stop bullying.

Things you might use

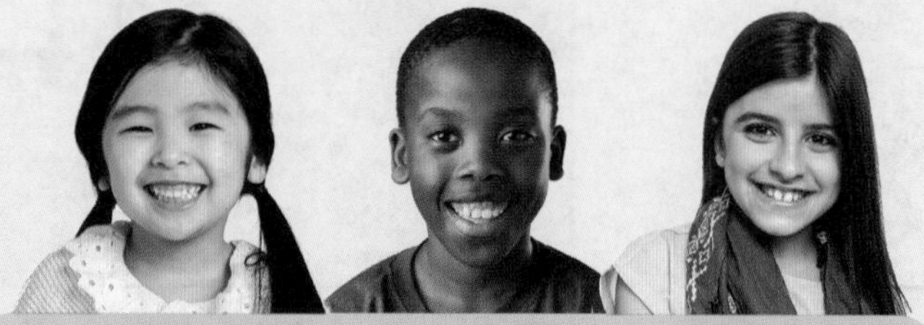
3 people to be in the play

Bully at School

Look at the picture. Then answer the items.

1. Tell about what you see happening in the picture.

____

____

2. Would you like to help? Why or why not?

____

____

3. What would you do if you were being bullied?

____

____

Skills:
Conduct research;
Make observations;
Use visual information;
Hypothesize;
Answer questions based on research

Bullying

Skills:
Use concepts to solve a non-routine problem;
Apply concepts;
Plan a story;
Create a solution to a problem;
Explain a design

Play Brainstorm

Brainstorm ideas for your play by writing and drawing pictures to answer the items.

Who are the characters in the play?

____

____

____

What is the problem in the play?

____

____

____

How does the problem get fixed?

____

____

____

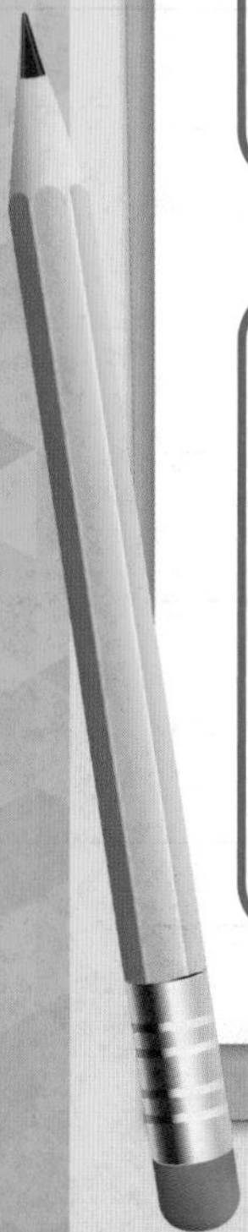

A Play to Help with Bullying

Write your play on a separate sheet of paper.

Then draw a picture and finish the sentences to tell more about your play.

This is what happens in the **beginning**: ______________________

____.

This is what happens in the **middle**: ______________________

____.

This is what happens in the **end**: ______________________

____.

Skills:
Create an original play;
Describe the major events in a play;
Draw or present visual information;
Evaluate a design;
Practice self-awareness

Bullying

Concepts:
It can be challenging to get used to new things;
It is important to try to understand different cultures;
Trying new things can be a good thing;
It is hard to move to a new place with a different culture;
Food is an important part of a culture

Read the story. Think about the problems in the story.

New Foods

Kapoor and his family moved from India to the United States. On his first day at the new school, the kids were nice to him. He made friends quickly. At lunchtime, Kapoor waited in line with his new friends. He saw trays with foods that he had never seen before. When Kapoor got his tray, he made a face. "This food does not look good. It does not smell like the food I like to eat back in India. I don't want it," Kapoor said.

"Just try it, you might like it," said his friend Dan. Kapoor closed his eyes as he bit into the pizza slice. He chewed it slowly at first. "It isn't bad, but I miss Indian food," said Kapoor. The next day he asked if he could have Indian food, but the cafeteria didn't have any. He missed India more every day.

On Friday morning, Kapoor smelled something yummy in his classroom. It was his favorite Indian dish! "Hello, class. Today we are celebrating cultures from around the world. We will be tasting food from different countries," said his teacher.

"Eww, what is that smell?" asked Dan. Kapoor laughed and explained that it was food from his country. "I guess it takes time for everybody to get used to something new."

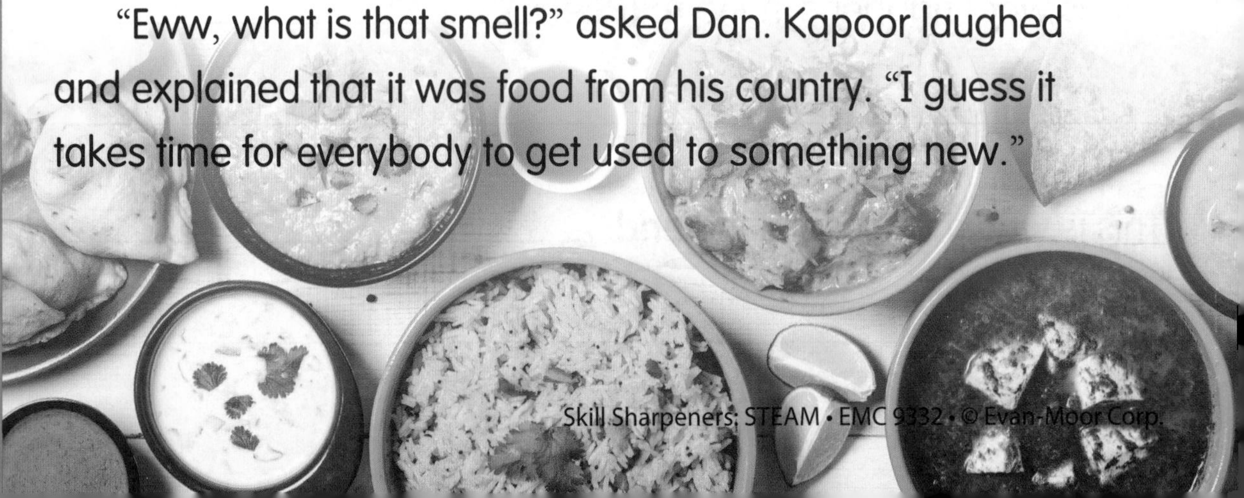

Problems with Lunch

Answer the items about the story you read.

1. Draw a picture of one problem you read about in the story. Then write a sentence about it.

One problem in the story is ______________________________

____.

2. What happened that made Kapoor feel better about living in the United States?

Kapoor felt better when ______________________________

____.

3. How would you feel if you could not eat the foods you like?

I would feel ______________________________

____.

Skills:

Identify key problems and ideas in a text;

Summarize a problem;

Empathize with a character in a story;

Produce a creative drawing to interpret a problem

School Lunches

School Lunches

Schools in the United States serve lunch to over 29 million students each day. Students come from different backgrounds, or cultures. Each culture eats different foods. This can make it hard for schools to make meals that all children like. Some children do not eat the foods that are served at school because they do not like them. They only like foods from their culture.

What Is Culture?

Culture is the way a group of people live their lives. Many things make up a group's culture. The way you dress, the language you speak, and what you believe makes up a culture. The foods you eat are a part of your culture, too.

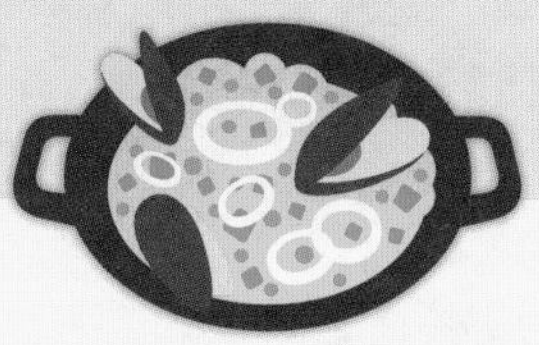

More Choices

Some schools serve lunches that have foods from different cultures. Schools ask parents from different cultures what meals they serve at home. This helps schools know more about foods from different cultures. Then they plan menus that have dishes from each culture.

Why Different Meals Matter

Some schools have students that used to live in different places around the world. When students move to a new place, they often miss their old homes. Eating a meal that they know and like may help new students feel more welcome.

Serving meals from around the world also teaches students about other cultures. Students learn that different cultures eat different foods. Learning about different cultures through school lunches can be fun.

Concepts:

Millions of school lunches are served on school days in the U.S.;

Some schools offer lunches with foods that represent different cultures;

Food can help teach us about different cultures

School Lunches

Skills:
Convey an idea through visual art;
Explore uses of materials and tools to create works of art or design;
Use observation and investigation in preparation for making a work of art;
Demonstrate creativity

Food Is Art

Making food is an art. Many chefs combine colorful foods and spices to make delicious dishes. The food not only tastes good, but it looks good on the plate, too.

Make your favorite snack look like a piece of art.

Step 1: Brainstorm

- What are your favorite snacks?
- How can you make your dish colorful?
- What tools will you need to make your dish?

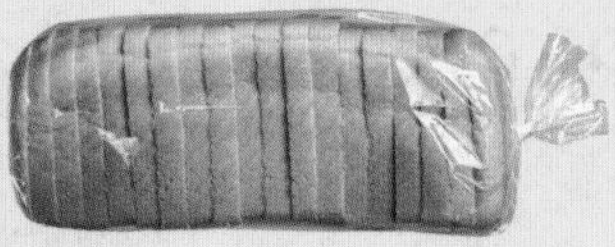

Step 2: Do Research

Think about these questions as you look at the pictures:

- Can you tell what the food art shows?
- Which dish do you like best, and why?
- Was it in a bowl or on a plate?
- Which foods were used?

School Lunches

Step 3: Plan

Choose the things you want to use.
These are things you might use:

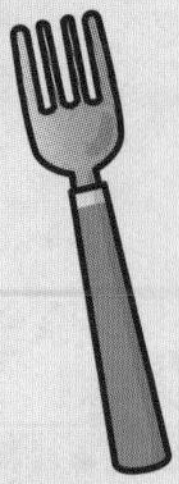

Draw what you would like to make on your plate.
Think about the foods you will use.

Step 4: Make It and Share It

Make your food art. Then take a picture of it or show it to a friend before you eat it!

School Lunches

Skills:
Sort foods into food groups;
Use visual information

A healthy school lunch has food from each of the 5 healthy food groups.

Look at the foods. Sort them into food groups. Write the name of each food on the line in its food group.

apple

carrots

chicken

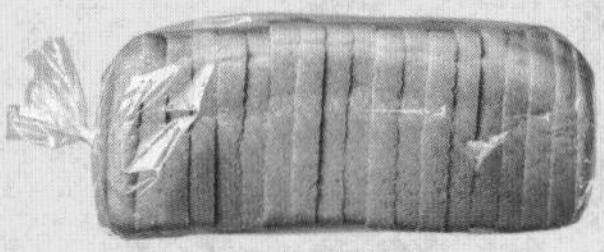
bread

milk

Dairy	Vegetables	Fruits
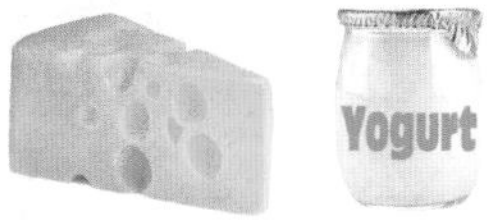 ______________	 ______________	 ______________

Meats and Eggs	Grains
 ______________	 ______________

School Lunches

Skills:

Sequence steps in a recipe;

Use visual information;

Recognize how technology can help us learn about and make foods from other cultures and teach others about foods from our own culture

Cooking with Technology

Technology can help you make different food. Pictures are a technology. Recipes sometimes have pictures to show you how to make the food. Television and videos are also technologies that you can use to watch how food is made.

Read. Look at the pictures. Number the recipe in order.

Lay vegetables, eggs, or meat on top of the rice.

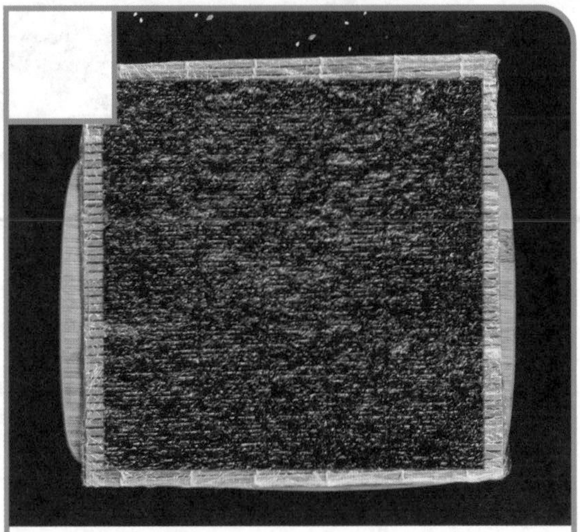

Place a piece of seaweed on the bamboo mat.

Use the bamboo mat to roll your sushi. Cut and enjoy!

Spread white rice over the seaweed.

Chef

A chef is a person who makes food. Chefs work in restaurants, hotels, schools, and many other places. A chef can cook many different foods.

Read about what people eat. Then read the menu choices. Draw a line to match each person to something he or she would like to eat.

I like to eat spicy foods.

I do not eat meat.

I love sandwiches.

Banh Mi

(Baun-Me)
Bread filled with fresh meat and vegetables

Hummus and Pita Bread

A vegetable and bean dip with flatbread

Jerk Chicken

Spicy chicken served with rice

Skills:

Learn about the career of chefs;

Use visual information;

Match descriptions to pictures;

Make inferences;

Read about foods from different cultures

School Lunches

STEAM Task

Problem & Task → **Research** → **Brainstorm & Design** → **Make It & Explain It**

Skills:
Problem solving;
Creative skills;
Solving problem-based, authentic tasks;
Multiple methods;
Multiple content areas;
Connected ideas;
Technology integration

School Lunches

Problem to Solve

Many students at your school come from different cultures. Some of them might feel like they don't belong at school because the school lunches do not include foods from their culture. Make a lunch menu poster with foods from different countries.

Task

First, do the research on the next page. Then brainstorm and design on page 102. Next, make the menu. Last, answer the items on page 103.

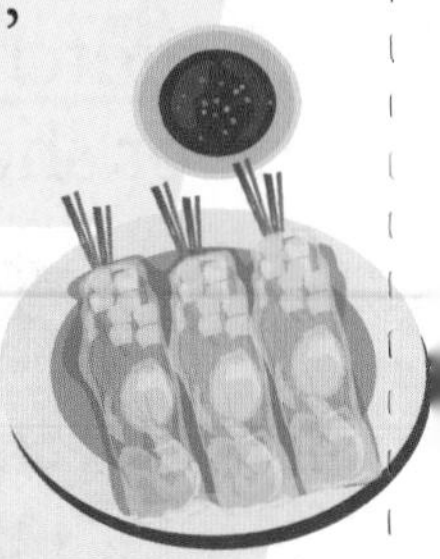

Rules

- The menu must include 3 different foods from 3 different countries.
- Your menu must have foods from each of the 5 food groups.

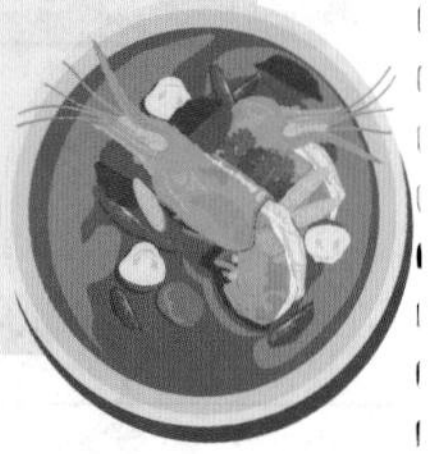

Things you might use

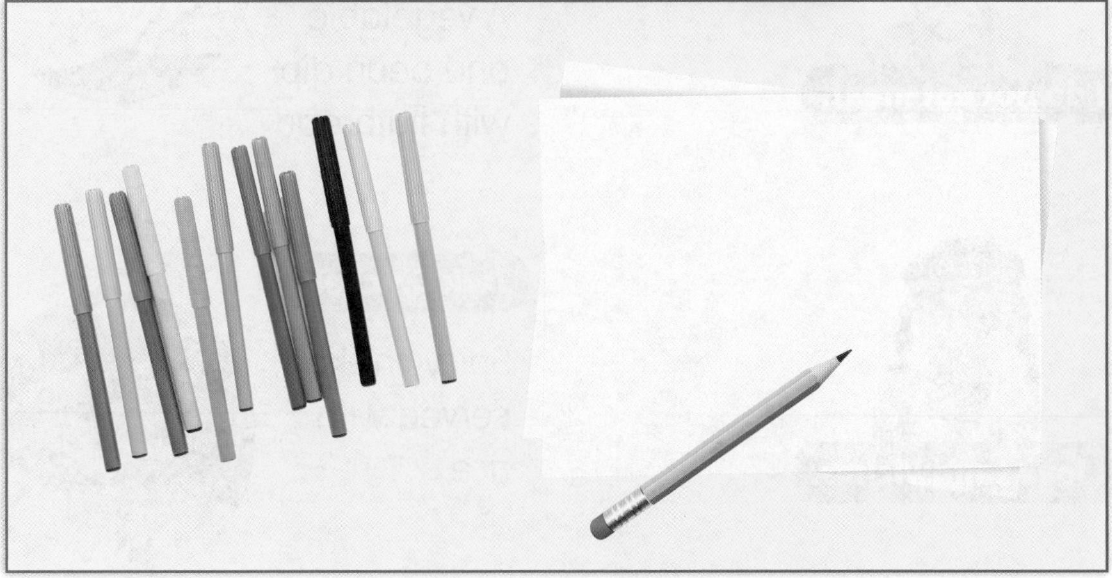

Food from Around the World

Skills:
Conduct research;
Make observations;
Use visual information;
Hypothesize;
Answer questions based on research

Read about food from different places in the world.
Look at the pictures.

USA

Cheeseburger:
Meat between two buns. Meat can be topped with cheese and vegetables.

Israel

Falafel:
Deep-fried dough made with herbs, spices, and smashed fava beans or chickpeas.

Mexico

Mole:
Thick sauce made with chilies and chocolate. Sauce can be served over rice, chicken, enchiladas, or other foods.

Russia

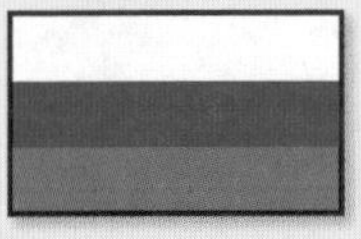

Pelmeni:
Dumplings made with dough and filled with meat.

Japan

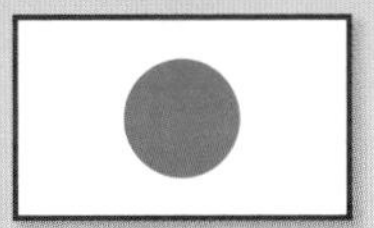

Sushi:
Rice and fish, usually raw. It can be made with vegetables and seaweed.

Vietnam

Pho:
Soup made with rice noodles, meat, and vegetables.

Problem & Task → Research → **Brainstorm & Design** → Make It & Explain It

Skills:

Use concepts to solve a non-routine problem;

Apply concepts;

Design a diverse lunch menu;

Create a solution to a problem;

Explain a design

Menu Brainstorm

Answer the items to help you brainstorm ideas for your menu.

Which foods from other countries would you like to try?

____

____

Now draw what you would like your menu poster to look like. Think about ways to get students to try new foods. Include items from each of the 5 food groups.

Make the Lunch Menu

Make your menu on a poster for all students to see.

Then draw a picture of your favorite food from your menu. Finish the sentences to tell more about your menu.

I made this special menu because ______________________________

____.

My favorite dish on the menu is ______________________________.

Skills:

Construct a lunch menu poster;

Explain the purpose of the menu;

Draw or present visual information;

Evaluate a design;

Practice self-awareness

Concepts:

People can be entertained using a wide variety of activities, tools, and games;

It can be disappointing when there is a power outage and we cannot use digital devices;

It is healthy to interact with other people sometimes by playing games

Read the story. Think about the problems in the story.

Fun Without a Screen

Mark called Pepo on the phone on Monday to ask if he wanted to play basketball. Pepo said, "No thanks" and played video games instead. Mark called him two more times during the week, but Pepo said no each time.

On Sunday, Pepo finally played basketball with Mark at the park. Mark ran up and down the court easily. But Pepo got tired quickly, so they did not play for long. The two boys left the park and made it to Mark's house before rain started to fall from the sky.

They played video games at Mark's house until they heard a big CRASH of thunder. Suddenly, all the power in the house turned off. The boys grabbed flashlights. "Oh no, what can we do now?" Pepo asked Mark. "Let's make up our own game," Mark replied as he ran out of the room. He came back with marbles, plastic cups, books, and a cereal box. "Let's try to roll the marbles down a ramp and into the cups. The person who rolls the most marbles into the cups wins!" Then Pepo said, "Sounds like fun!" as he stacked the books. Mark and Pepo had fun all night playing with the ramp.

Pepo's Problems

Answer the items about the story you read.

1. Draw a picture of one problem you read about in the story. Then write a sentence about it.

One problem in the story is ______________________________

____.

2. Why do you think Pepo felt tired so quickly when he played basketball?

I think Pepo felt tired quickly because ____________________

____.

3. What did Mark do that may change Pepo's mind about spending so much of his time playing video games?

____

____

Skills:
Identify key problems and ideas in a text;
Summarize a problem;
Make inferences;
Produce a creative drawing to interpret a problem

Screen Time

Watching TV and playing video games can be fun. Sometimes, what you watch and what you play using technology can be educational and help you learn. But did you know that sitting and looking at a screen for a long time can be bad for your health? Some doctors say that people need to think about how much time they spend on a screen and how much time they spend being active and moving their bodies.

What Counts as Screen Time

Screen time is the amount of time you spend looking at a screen on a piece of technology. Some doctors believe children should have screen time for 2 hours or less each day. But many children spend 3 hours or more in front of a screen.

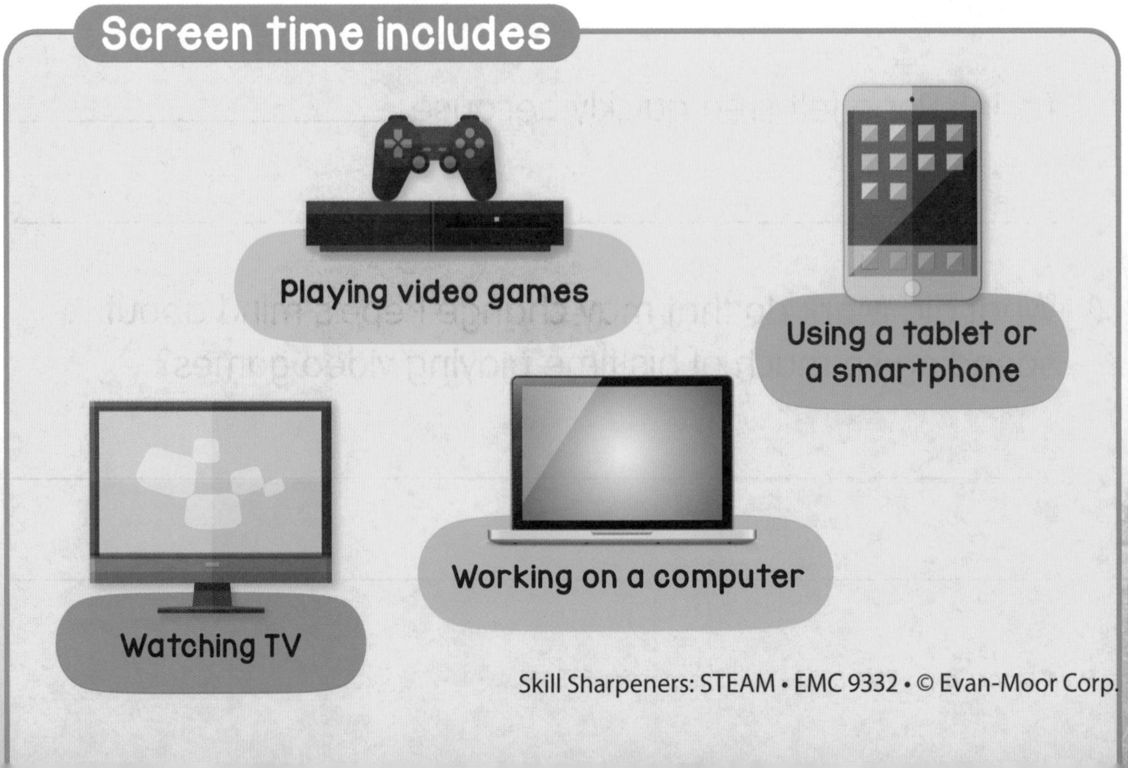

Some doctors believe that too much screen time can hurt your body in different ways. For example, this is what too much screen time can do:

- It can prevent you from getting enough exercise. Your body needs to move around and get exercise to stay healthy.
- It can hurt your eyes. Looking at a screen for too long can make it harder to see over time.
- It can cause pain in your fingers, wrists, back, and neck.
- It can make it hard to go to sleep. The glow from a screen can make it hard for some people's bodies to relax.

Other Ways to Have Fun

Screen time can be fun, but it is also important to do things that are not in front of a screen. Activities like dancing, playing sports, and bike riding can also be fun and keep you healthy. But if you like to play games, you can make up your own games with things you have around the house. You can roll a ball through a tower of paper cups. You can draw boxes on the sidewalk to play hopscotch. You can even grab items from your kitchen and catapult marshmallows onto a target!

Concepts:

A balance of screen time and off-screen time is recommended for our health;

Competitive and social games are good for our health

Skills:

Convey an idea through visual art;

Use observation and investigation in preparation for making a work of art;

Demonstrate creativity

Guess Who!

Pablo Picasso is a famous painter from the early 1900s. People and objects in his paintings looked as if they were broken into pieces and put back together in unusual ways.

Picasso-style art

You can make your own Picasso-style art by playing this game. The object of the game is for you to draw a family member or a friend in Picasso's style. Then your family or friends must guess who it is. All you need is scissors, a pencil, and crayons.

How to Play

1. First, pick one friend or family member to draw.
2. Then cut out the number cards on page 109. Mix them up and place them facedown.
3. Next, you will have 4 turns to pick a card. After you pick a card for your 1st turn, look at the Picasso table on page 109. Find the body part that matches the number you picked for the 1st turn. Draw that body part on page 110.
4. Now pick a card for your 2nd turn. Repeat what you did until you draw a body part. Then do your 3rd turn and 4th turn so that you draw all the face parts.
5. Add hair and other things to your picture. Color it.
6. Last, show your art to friends or family members and have them guess who you drew!

These pictures were not made by Picasso but show Picasso-style art.

	1st Turn Draw a face	2nd Turn Draw a nose	3rd Turn Draw eyes	4th Turn Draw a mouth
1				
2				
3	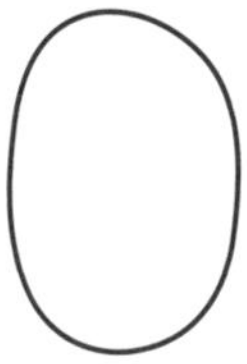			
4	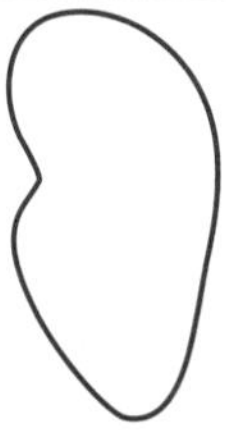			
5	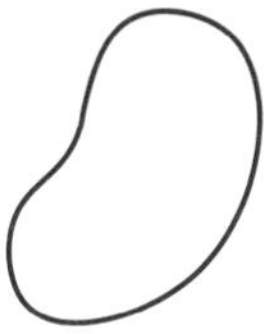			
6	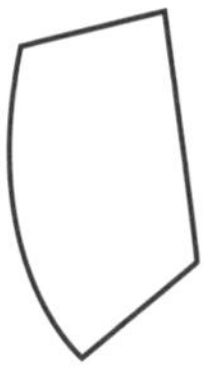			

1	2	3	4	5	6

My Picasso Art

Healthy Fun

You can stay healthy by balancing how much time you spend looking at a screen and how much time you spend doing activities that keep your body moving and exercising.

Skills:
Make inferences;
Use visual information;
Recognize activities that provide exercise

Read how each child spends his or her screen time. Then circle an activity that matches what that child might like to do.

1. Amanda watches videos about animals and nature on her computer.

go on a hike

jump rope

2. Ben drives fast cars in his favorite video game called Speed Racer.

do yoga

ride a bike

3. Will likes to watch music videos on his tablet.

play soccer

dance

Skills:
Add;
Solve a word problem;
Compare numbers;
Use visual information

Keeping Score

Some games have only one winner at the end of the game. Keeping score helps you know who wins the game.

Luke and Clay are playing a new game called Bag Toss. They toss 3 beanbags into a bucket. Each bucket is worth 5, 10, or 20 points. The player with the most points at the end wins!

Look at the points each bucket is worth. Then look at the buckets below each player. Add up their points. Then write who won the game.

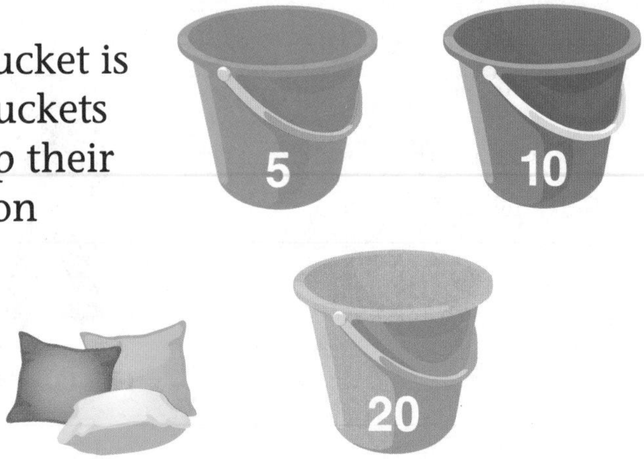

Luke

Score: ______

Clay

Score: ______

The winner is

____

Board Game Designer

A board game designer is a person who makes and designs board games for people to play.

Skills:

Use visual information;

Learn about the job of board game designers;

Write creative text for a board game

Help the designer finish the board game. Finish the sentences in each space.

Silly Willy

Let's get silly with Willy the Caterpillar! Roll the die, move your game piece, and do the action given on that space. Reach the end first to win!

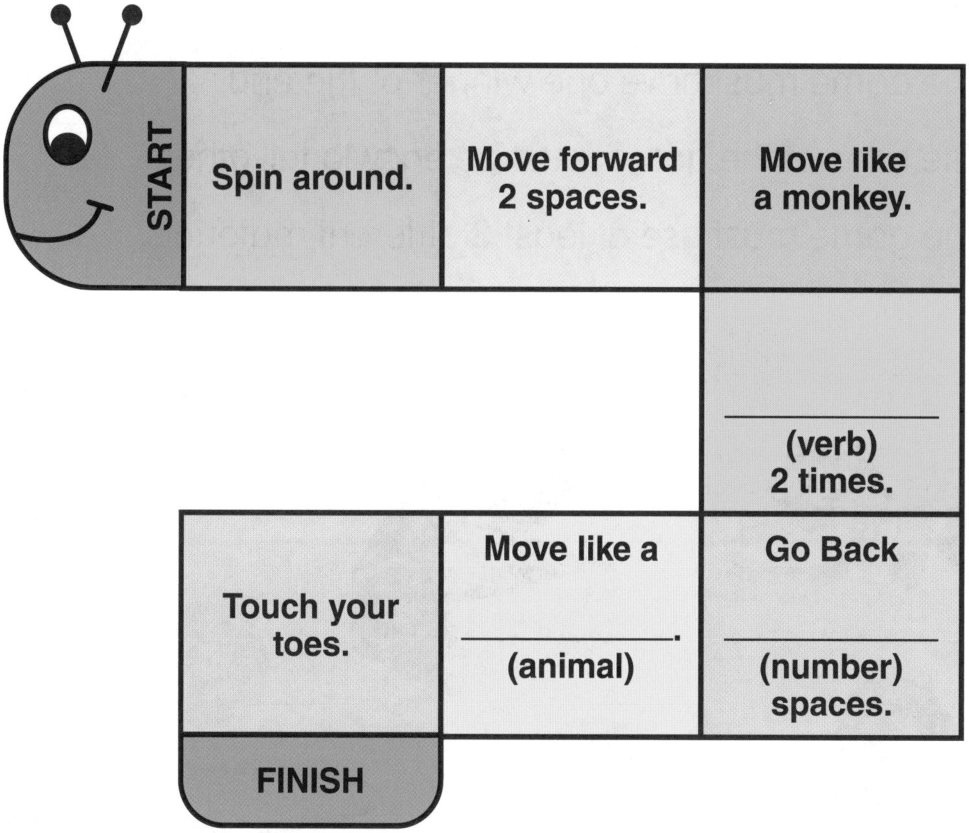

Skills:
Problem solving;
Creative skills;
Solving problem-based, authentic tasks;
Multiple methods;
Multiple content areas;
Connected ideas;
Technology integration

Problem to Solve

You and your friends are having fun playing your favorite video game at lunchtime. But suddenly, the power goes out! Now you and your friends need something fun to play. You will make a fun game using things around your house.

Task

First, do the research on the next page. Then brainstorm and design on page 116. Next, make and play your game. Last, answer the items on page 117.

Rules

- The game must have one winner at the end.
- The rules of the game must be easy to tell others.
- The game must use at least 3 different materials.

Things you might use

Homemade Fun

Read. Look at the pictures. Then answer the items.

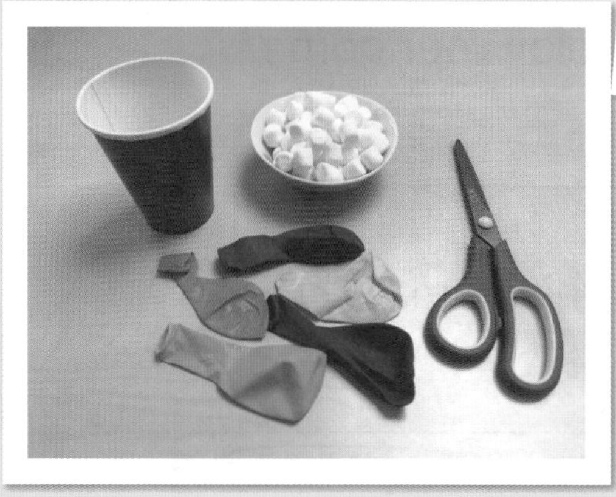

This game is called Marshmallow Shooter. A slingshot is made from a plastic cup and a balloon. You put marshmallows inside the cup, pull back on the balloon, and watch your marshmallows shoot out! You use chalk to draw circles on the ground. In the game, you try to shoot the marshmallows into the circles. The person who shoots the most marshmallows into the circles wins!

1. What materials did the children use to make this game?

____

2. Are the rules of the game easy to learn?

____

3. How do you win this game?

____

Skills:

Conduct research;

Use visual information;

Make observations;

Answer questions based on text and visual information

Problem & Task → Research → **Brainstorm & Design** → Make It & Explain It

Skills:
Use concepts to solve a non-routine problem;
Apply concepts;
Design a game;
Create a solution to a problem;
Explain a design;
Use creative thinking;
Formulate rules;
Brainstorm and draw

Game Brainstorm

Answer the items to help you brainstorm ideas for your game.

1. What things do you need to play your game?

___

2. How many people can play this game?

___

3. How do you win this game?

___

Now draw a picture of what your game will look like. Think about what you will use.

Game Time

Make and play the game you made up.

Glue or draw a picture of you playing the game.

Finish the sentences to tell more about your game.

My game is called ______________________________.

This is how you play:

____

____

______________________________.

Skills:

Create an original game;

Formulate and explain the rules of an original game;

Draw or present visual information;

Evaluate a design

Concepts:
Sometimes storms are severe and can change the way we live our lives;
It is helpful to be prepared with supplies for natural disasters and weather events;
It can be challenging when electric power goes out and school is canceled

Emergency Kit

Read the story. Think about the problems in the story.

Ready for a Snow Day

Kendall woke up and ran to the computer. Her brother was already there checking to see if their school had declared it a snow day. "Yes!" said her brother Steve, "Another snow day!" "Oh no," thought Kendall, "not another snow day!" Kendall loved school and this was the third snow day in a row. There was a big blizzard, and all the roads were closed. They still had lights and water, but sometimes when the winds got really strong, they lost both water and electricity.

Kendall hoped that wouldn't happen again this time, but if it did, she was going to be prepared! Kendall grabbed a shoebox and started putting things inside it. She put in a flashlight, a water bottle, granola bars, a pair of warm mittens, and a hat. "Sometimes, my phone doesn't work in a heavy storm. How can I call for help?" asked Kendall.

"Use this whistle," said Steve. "Blow it to make a loud sound and signal for help." Kendall smiled and said, "Great idea! Now I'm ready for the next snow day."

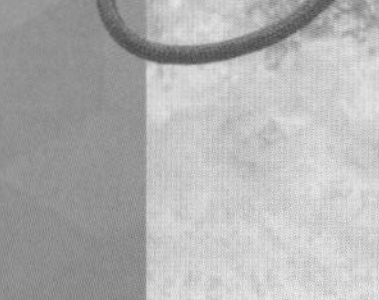

Snowed In

Skills:
Identify key problems and ideas in a text;
Summarize a problem;
Formulate solutions to problems;
Produce a creative drawing to interpret a problem

Answer the items about the story you read.

1. Draw a picture of one problem you read about in the story. Then write a sentence about it.

One problem in the story is ______________________________

____.

2. Why did Kendall put things in a shoebox?

She put things in a shoebox because ______________________

____.

3. What other things should Kendall put in her shoebox?

She can put ______________________________________

______________________________________ in her box.

Emergency Kit

Snow Days

Snow can be a lot of fun to play in. You can sled down snowy hills. You can make a snowman or have a snowball fight. But too much snow at one time can be unsafe. Being prepared can help you and your family stay safe when there is a bad storm.

What Snowstorms Bring

When there is a lot of snowfall and strong winds, it is called a snowstorm. Snow can pile so high on the ground that you cannot walk or drive on the streets. Piles of snow can be taller than you! Schools cancel classes because teachers and students cannot travel to school. Stores selling food and supplies are closed, too.

Strong winds in a snowstorm can make the power go out. We need power to turn on the lights in our houses, use the Internet, and use our telephones.

Be Prepared

It is important to be prepared for a snowstorm. You may not know when a big storm is coming. Stay safe in the next snowstorm by keeping all the things you need in a safety kit.

Here are some things you might pack in your snowstorm safety kit:

- [ ] Things to keep you warm, such as a blanket, hat, and mittens.
- [ ] Water and food that will last a long time, like canned food or peanut butter.
- [ ] A flashlight with extra batteries will help you see in the dark if the power goes out.
- [ ] A cellphone and a charger for the cellphone to call for help. Also pack other tools, such as a whistle or a radio, in case you can't use a cellphone to call for help.
- [ ] A first-aid kit with bandages in case someone gets hurt.
- [ ] If you have pets, pack food and water for them, too.

Concepts:

Emergency kits can help people be prepared for severe weather events or natural disasters;

Natural events can affect how people live their lives

Skills:
Create visual art with a purpose and to convey information;
Demonstrate creativity;
Follow directions

Emergency Kit

It is important to be prepared for an emergency. Stay safe by packing what you need in an emergency kit.

Make a pretend emergency kit to show your family. Then make a real one together.

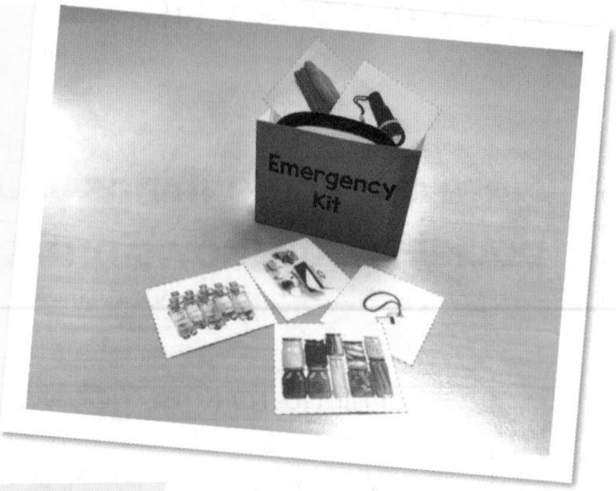

What you need for the art project:

- cutouts on page 123
- scissors
- glue

What you need for the real emergency kit:

- shoebox or backpack
- different emergency items

What You Do

1. First, cut out the emergency kit bag on page 123.
2. Next, fold the bag so it stands up, then glue the side flaps together.
3. Then cut out the other items on page 123 and put them inside the bag.
4. Last, use your pretend emergency kit for ideas on what you will need in your real one. Grab a shoebox or a backpack and fill it up!

Emergency Kit

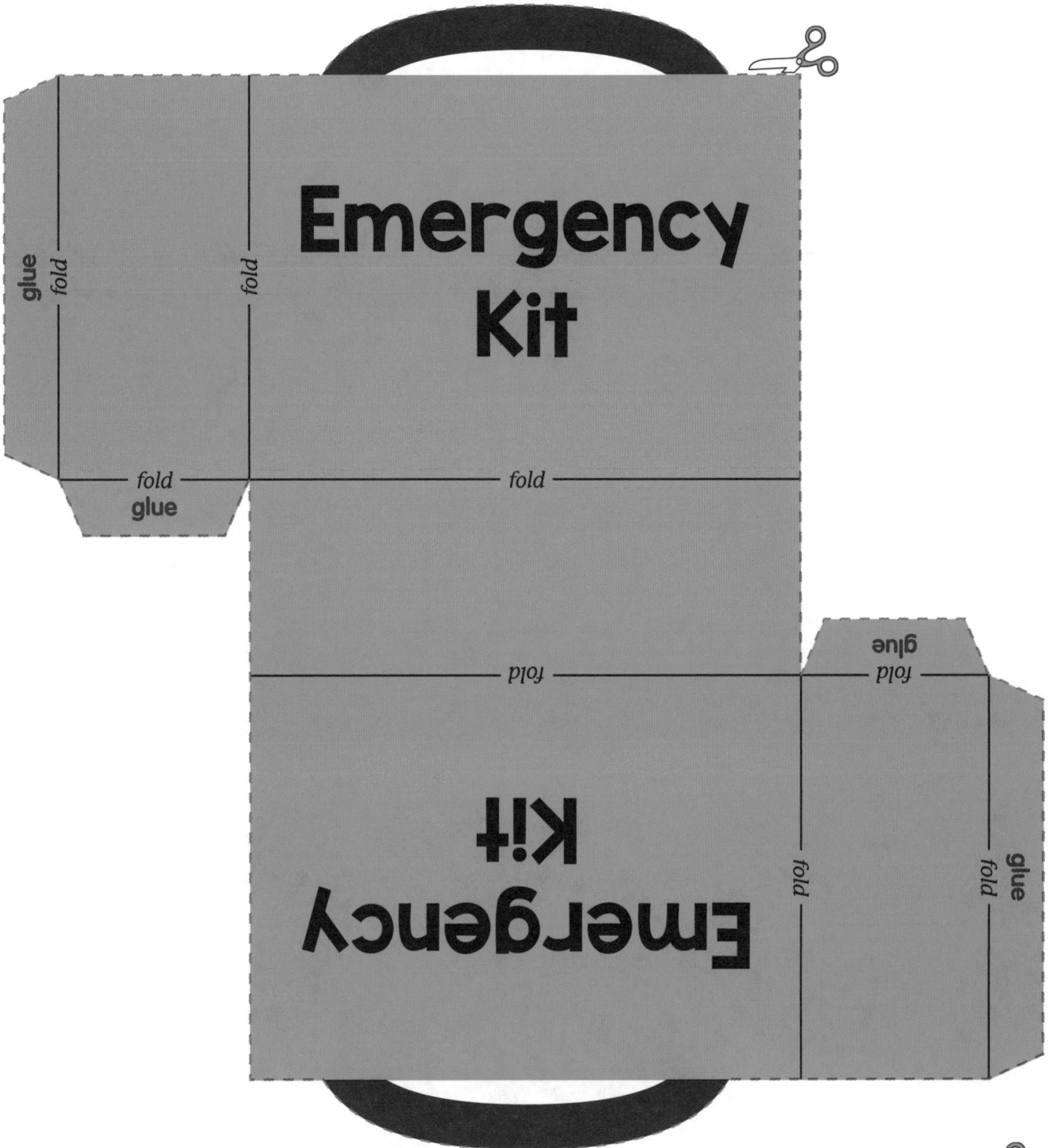
Emergency
Kit
glue
fold
fold
fold
glue
fold
fold
glue
fold
fold
glue
Emergency
Kit

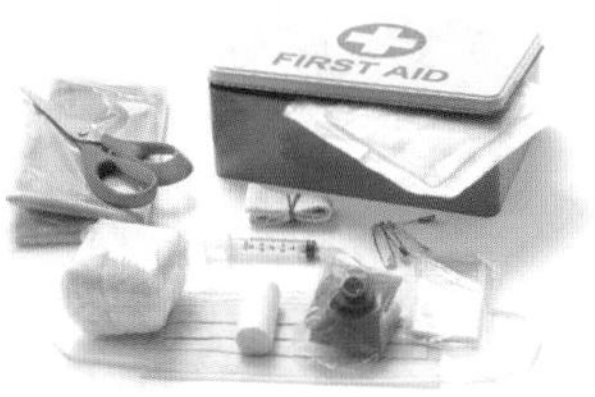
FIRST AID

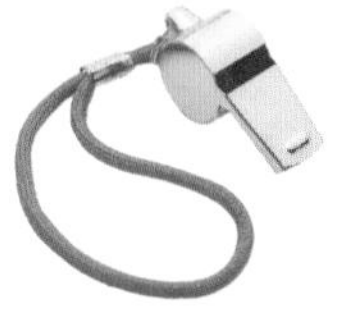

Food and Water for the Storm

Sometimes when a big storm hits, you cannot go out for supplies. It is important to have enough supplies for everyone in your house.

Skills:
Solve a word problem;
Add or multiply;
Represent data on a bar graph

Answer the items.

1. Calvin, his mom, and his sister need to prepare for a storm that will last 3 days. Each of them needs 1 gallon of water a day. How much water does his family need to have for the storm?

   _____ gallons of water

Show Your Work

2. Count the food items. Color one square for each item.

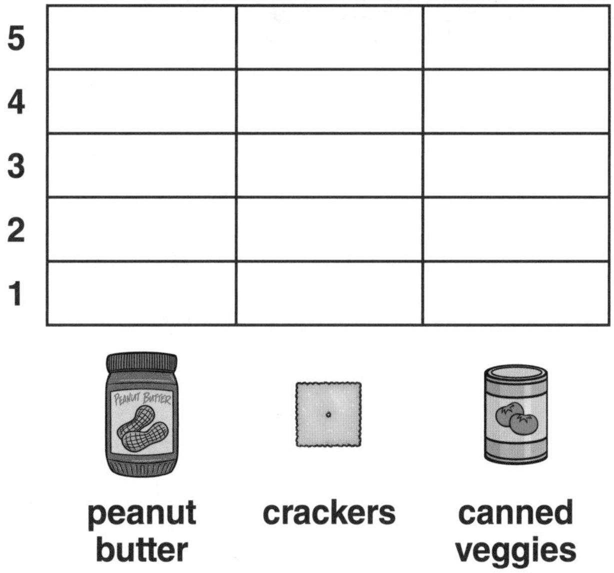

Skills:
Learn about solar energy;
Recognize that engineers work to solve problems;
Produce drawings to convey information;
Recognize ways people can use solar energy

No Power

The power can go out during an emergency. For some people, that means no heat and no electricity. But engineers have found a way to use the sun's light to make power for the things people need.

This device uses sunlight to charge a phone.

This oven uses solar power to cook food.

Solar panels on top of this house use sunlight to make electricity to turn on the lights.

What other things can we use solar power for? Draw them.

First Responder

A first responder is a person who is trained to help others when they are in trouble. First responders can help people who are stuck in a snowstorm.

© Rob Wilson / Shutterstock.com

Skills:
Learn about the careers of first responders in emergency situations;
Match pictures to descriptions;
Use visual information;
Use context clues

Draw a line to match.

Police officer

Firefighter

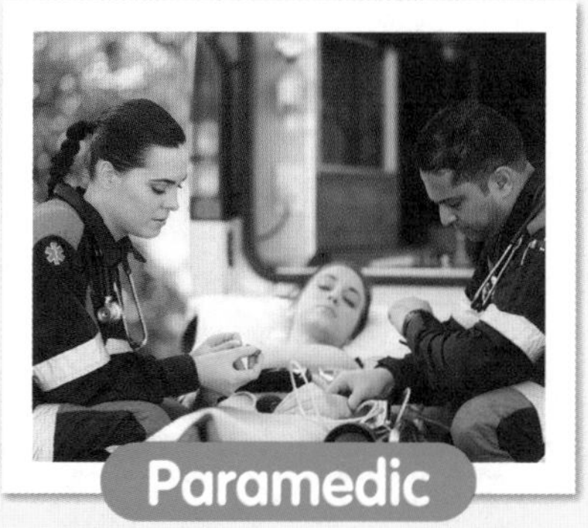
Paramedic

- a person who puts out fires and rescues others
- a health care worker who helps sick and hurt people
- a person who stops crime and protects the public

Skills:
Problem solving;
Creative skills;
Solving problem-based, authentic tasks;
Multiple methods;
Multiple content areas;
Connected ideas;

Problem to Solve

The weather forecaster has predicted that a big storm is coming. Some people do not know how to prepare for a snowstorm. Your job is to make a 3-D poster that will show people how to prepare for the storm.

Task

First, do the research on the next page to find out what can happen to people during a snowstorm. Then brainstorm and design on page 130. Last, make your 3-D poster and answer the items on page 131.

Rule

- The poster must show at least three 3-D things people will need to do to stay safe in a snowstorm.

Things you might use

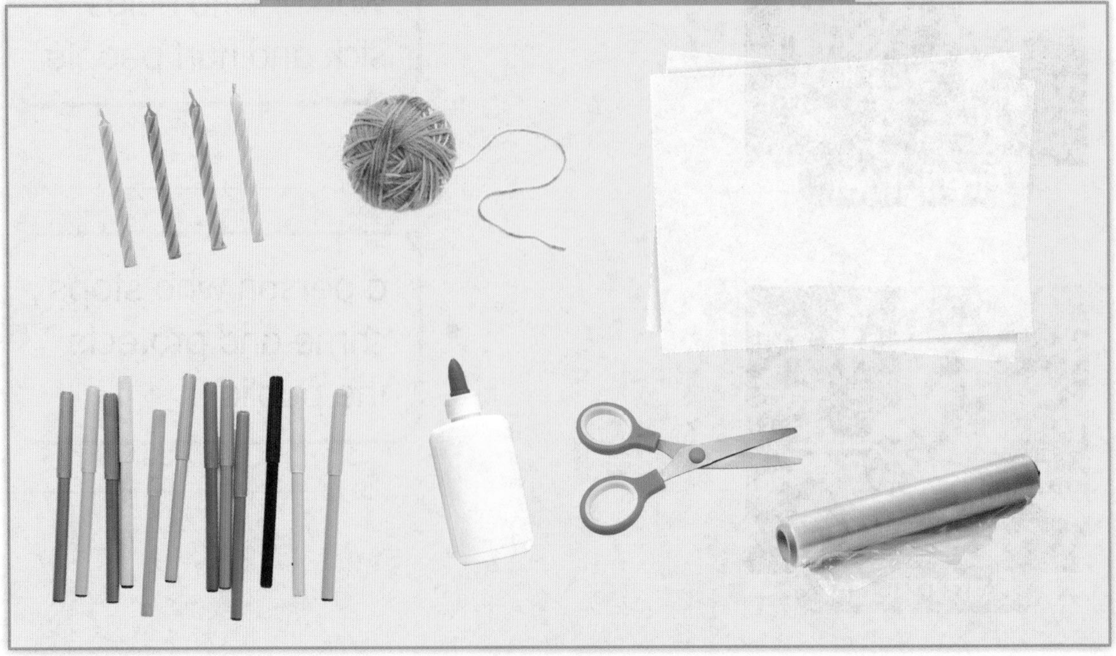

Snowstorm Trouble

Skills:
Conduct research;
Make observations;
Use visual information;
Answer questions based on research;
Make inferences

Look at the pictures. Read about the problems some people can have during a snowstorm.

People can freeze if they do not have heat or something to keep them warm.

Snowstorms can make it hard to travel to the store to buy food and water.

Snowstorms can make the power go out. Then houses do not have electricity or lights for people to use.

Write another problem people can have during a snowstorm.

____

____

Skills:
Use concepts to solve a non-routine problem;
Apply concepts;
Design an informative poster;
Develop a logical plan;
Create a solution to a problem;
Explain a design

Poster Brainstorm

Answer the items to help you brainstorm what to put on your poster.

1. Why is it important to prepare for a snowstorm?

2. What items would you pack in an emergency kit?

3. What can you pack in your emergency kit that will be fun and keep you from being bored?

Now draw a picture of what you want to put on your poster.

Problem & Task → Research → Brainstorm & Design → **Make It & Explain It**

Preparing for a Snowstorm Poster

Make your poster. Take a picture of it or draw it in the box. Then finish the sentences to tell more about it.

Skills:
Create a poster that informs about preparing for a severe weather event;
Explain the function of the poster;
Draw or present visual information

I made my poster to help others ______________________________

____.

These are 3 things people can do to get ready for a snowstorm:

1. ______________________________
2. ______________________________
3. ______________________________

Congratulations!

____

Name

You solved STEAM problems!

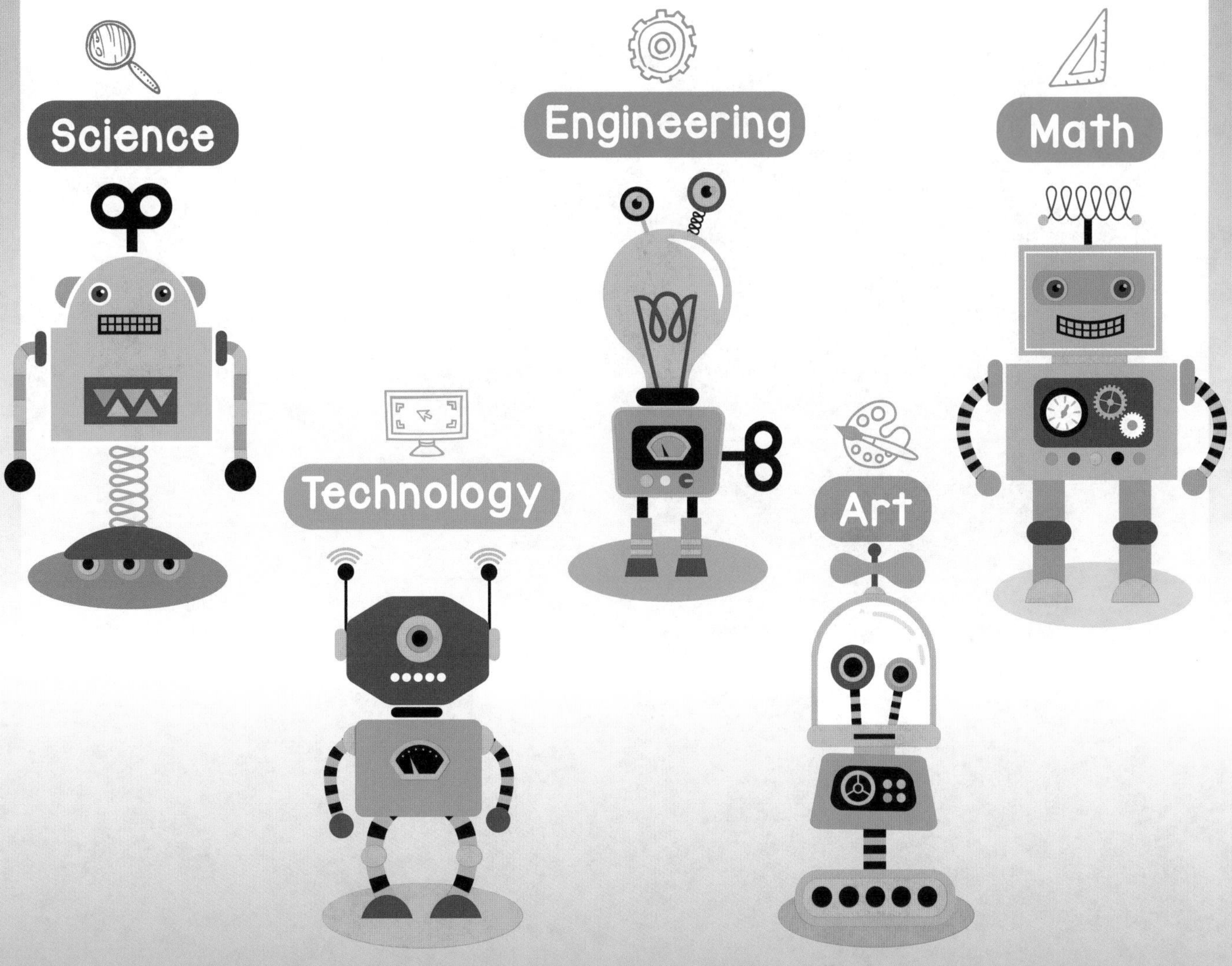

Cut out the pieces. Put them together to find out what the picture shows. Then glue them onto construction paper to make a poster.

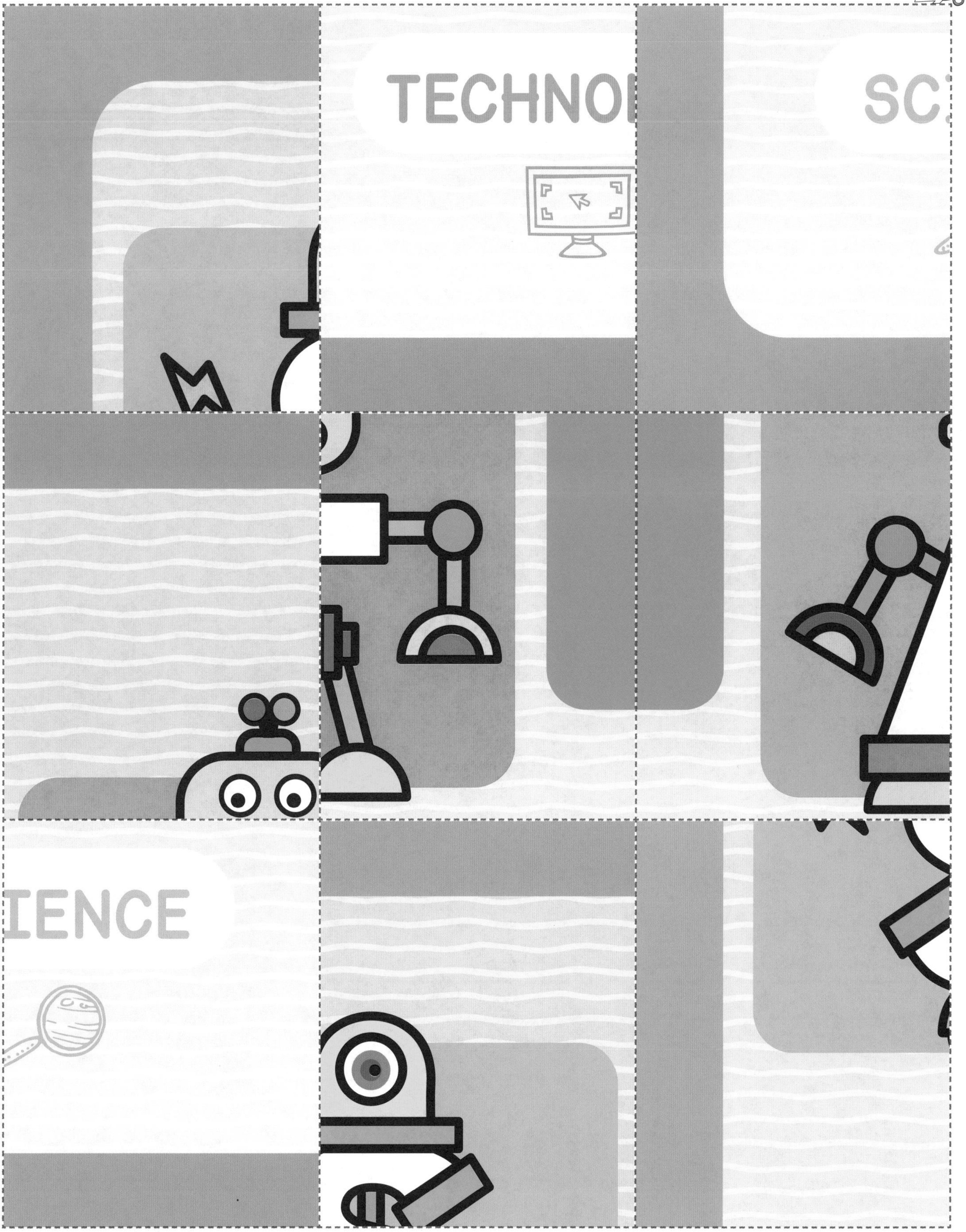

NGINEERIN
NG
LOGY
EN

ART
MATHEMA
ATICS

Puzzle size 22" × 9"

Answer Key

Page 7

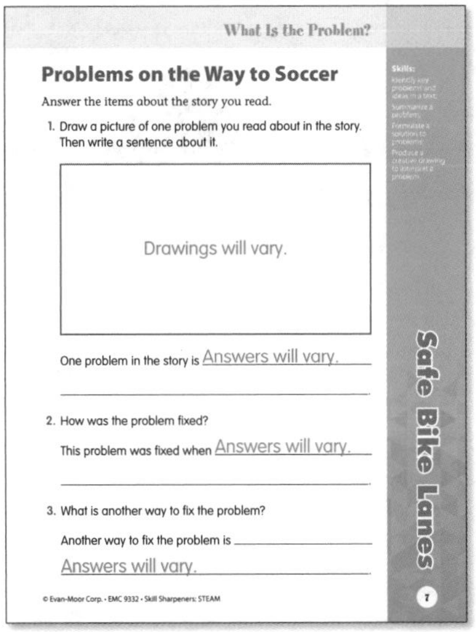
What Is the Problem?

Problems on the Way to Soccer

Answer the items about the story you read.

1. Draw a picture of one problem you read about in the story. Then write a sentence about it.

Drawings will vary.

One problem in the story is Answers will vary.

2. How was the problem fixed?

This problem was fixed when Answers will vary.

3. What is another way to fix the problem?

Another way to fix the problem is Answers will vary.

Safe Bike Lanes

© Evan-Moor Corp. • EMC 9332 • Skill Sharpeners: STEAM 7

Page 13

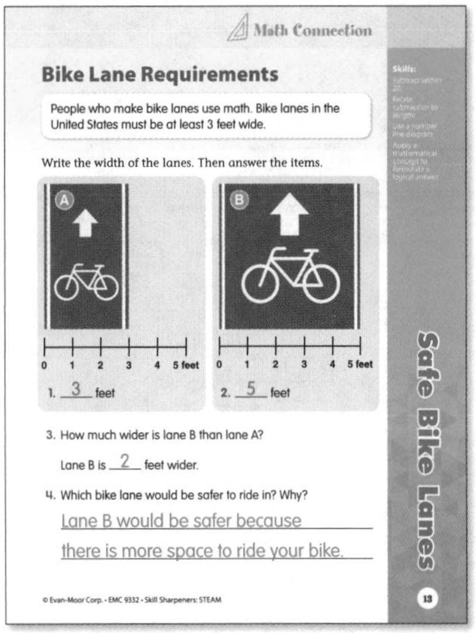
Math Connection

Bike Lane Requirements

People who make bike lanes use math. Bike lanes in the United States must be at least 3 feet wide.

Write the width of the lanes. Then answer the items.

1. 3 feet

2. 5 feet

3. How much wider is lane B than lane A?

Lane B is 2 feet wider.

4. Which bike lane would be safer to ride in? Why?

Lane B would be safer because there is more space to ride your bike.

Safe Bike Lanes

© Evan-Moor Corp. • EMC 9332 • Skill Sharpeners: STEAM 13

Page 14

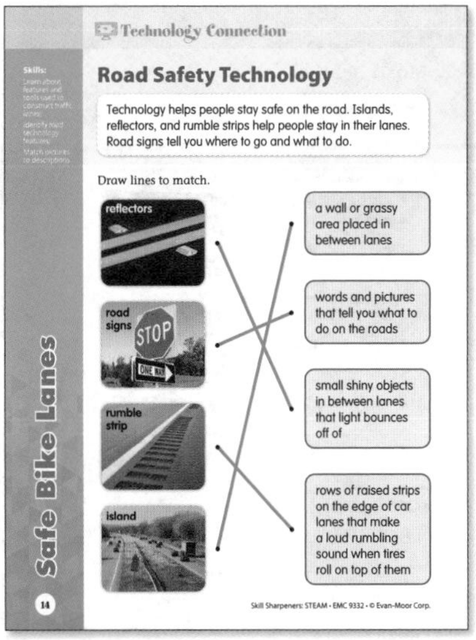
Technology Connection

Road Safety Technology

Technology helps people stay safe on the road. Islands, reflectors, and rumble strips help people stay in their lanes. Road signs tell you where to go and what to do.

Draw lines to match.

reflectors — small shiny objects in between lanes that light bounces off of

road signs — words and pictures that tell you what to do on the roads

rumble strip — rows of raised strips on the edge of car lanes that make a loud rumbling sound when tires roll on top of them

island — a wall or grassy area placed in between lanes

Safe Bike Lanes

14 Skill Sharpeners: STEAM • EMC 9332 • © Evan-Moor Corp.

Page 15

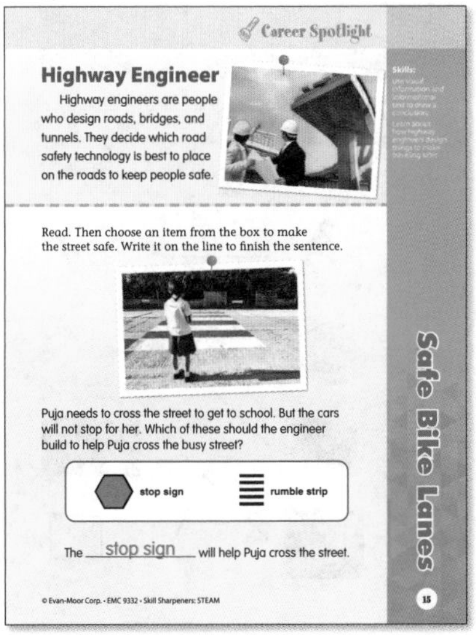
Career Spotlight

Highway Engineer

Highway engineers are people who design roads, bridges, and tunnels. They decide which road safety technology is best to place on the roads to keep people safe.

Read. Then choose an item from the box to make the street safe. Write it on the line to finish the sentence.

Puja needs to cross the street to get to school. But the cars will not stop for her. Which of these should the engineer build to help Puja cross the busy street?

stop sign | rumble strip

The stop sign will help Puja cross the street.

Safe Bike Lanes

© Evan-Moor Corp. • EMC 9332 • Skill Sharpeners: STEAM 15

Page 21

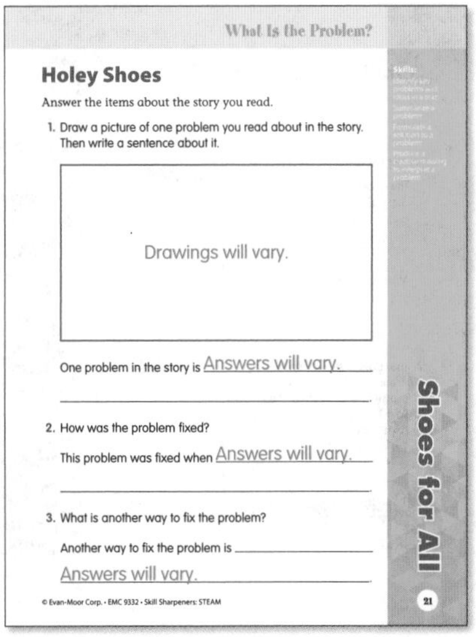
What Is the Problem?

Holey Shoes

Answer the items about the story you read.

1. Draw a picture of one problem you read about in the story. Then write a sentence about it.

Drawings will vary.

One problem in the story is Answers will vary.

2. How was the problem fixed?

This problem was fixed when Answers will vary.

3. What is another way to fix the problem?

Another way to fix the problem is Answers will vary.

Shoes for All

© Evan-Moor Corp. • EMC 9332 • Skill Sharpeners: STEAM 21

Page 27

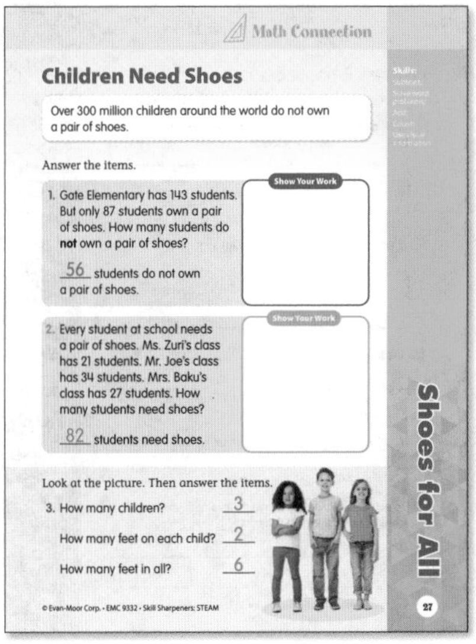
Math Connection

Children Need Shoes

Over 300 million children around the world do not own a pair of shoes.

Answer the items.

1. Gate Elementary has 143 students. But only 87 students own a pair of shoes. How many students do **not** own a pair of shoes?

56 students do not own a pair of shoes.

2. Every student at school needs a pair of shoes. Ms. Zuri's class has 21 students. Mr. Joe's class has 34 students. Mrs. Baku's class has 27 students. How many students need shoes?

82 students need shoes.

Show Your Work

Look at the picture. Then answer the items.

3. How many children? 3

How many feet on each child? 2

How many feet in all? 6

Shoes for All

© Evan-Moor Corp. • EMC 9332 • Skill Sharpeners: STEAM 27

Page 28

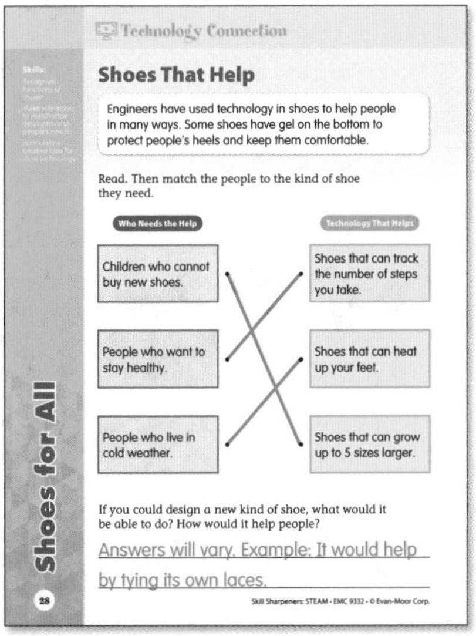
Technology Connection

Shoes That Help

Engineers have used technology in shoes to help people in many ways. Some shoes have gel on the bottom to protect people's heels and keep them comfortable.

Read. Then match the people to the kind of shoe they need.

Who Needs the Help — Technology That Helps

Children who cannot buy new shoes. — Shoes that can grow up to 5 sizes larger.

People who want to stay healthy. — Shoes that can track the number of steps you take.

People who live in cold weather. — Shoes that can heat up your feet.

If you could design a new kind of shoe, what would it be able to do? How would it help people?

Answers will vary. Example: It would help by tying its own laces.

Shoes for All

28 Skill Sharpeners: STEAM • EMC 9332 • © Evan-Moor Corp.

Page 29

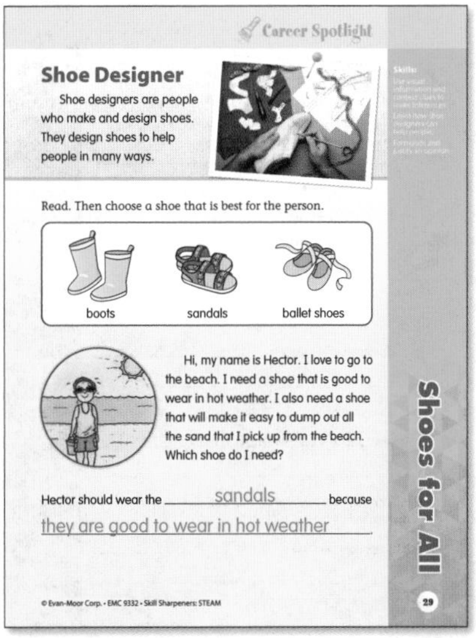
Career Spotlight

Shoe Designer

Shoe designers are people who make and design shoes. They design shoes to help people in many ways.

Read. Then choose a shoe that is best for the person.

boots | sandals | ballet shoes

Hi, my name is Hector. I love to go to the beach. I need a shoe that is good to wear in hot weather. I also need a shoe that will make it easy to dump out all the sand that I pick up from the beach. Which shoe do I need?

Hector should wear the sandals because they are good to wear in hot weather.

Shoes for All

© Evan-Moor Corp. • EMC 9332 • Skill Sharpeners: STEAM 29

Page 35

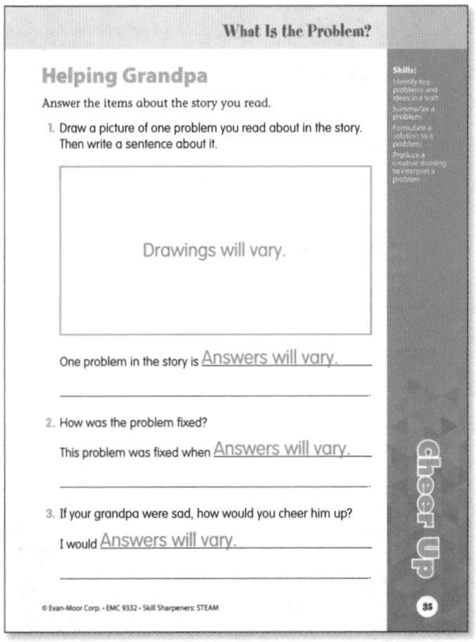
What Is the Problem?

Helping Grandpa

Answer the items about the story you read.

1. Draw a picture of one problem you read about in the story. Then write a sentence about it.

Drawings will vary.

One problem in the story is Answers will vary.

2. How was the problem fixed?

This problem was fixed when Answers will vary.

3. If your grandpa were sad, how would you cheer him up?

I would Answers will vary.

Cheer Up

© Evan-Moor Corp. • EMC 9332 • Skill Sharpeners: STEAM 35

Page 41

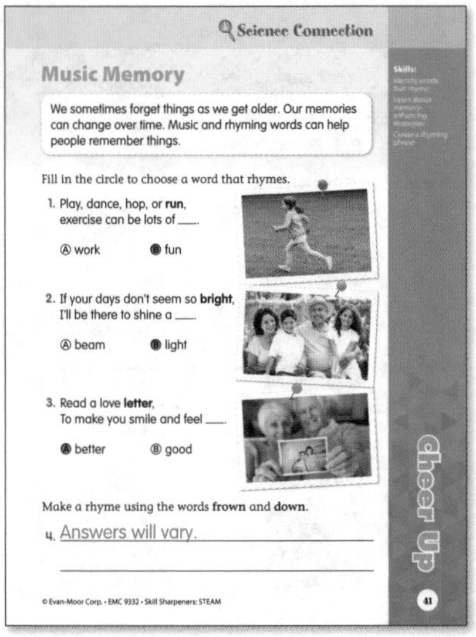
Science Connection

Music Memory

We sometimes forget things as we get older. Our memories can change over time. Music and rhyming words can help people remember things.

Fill in the circle to choose a word that rhymes.

1. Play, dance, hop, or **run**, exercise can be lots of ____.
   Ⓐ work ● fun
2. If your days don't seem so **bright**, I'll be there to shine a ____.
   Ⓐ beam ● light
3. Read a love **letter**, To make you smile and feel ____.
   ● better Ⓑ good

Make a rhyme using the words **frown** and **down**.

4. Answers will vary.

Cheer Up

© Evan-Moor Corp. • EMC 9332 • Skill Sharpeners: STEAM 41

Page 42

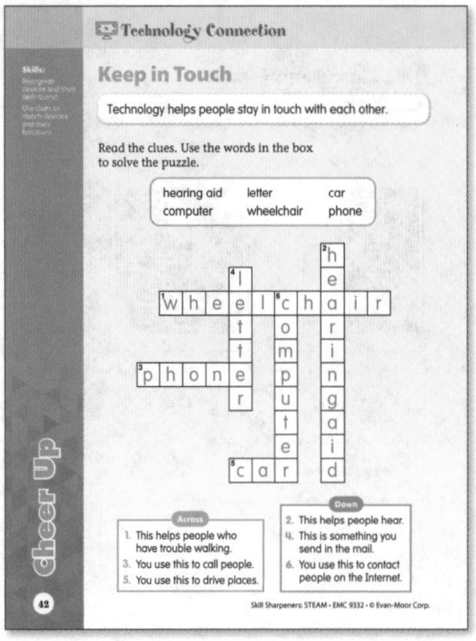
Technology Connection

Keep in Touch

Technology helps people stay in touch with each other.

Read the clues. Use the words in the box to solve the puzzle.

hearing aid letter car computer wheelchair phone

Across: 1. wheelchair 3. phone 5. car
Down: 2. hearing aid 4. letter 6. computer

Across
1. This helps people who have trouble walking.
3. You use this to call people.
5. You use this to drive places.

Down
2. This helps people hear.
4. This is something you send in the mail.
6. You use this to contact people on the Internet.

Cheer Up

42 Skill Sharpeners: STEAM • EMC 9332 • © Evan-Moor Corp.

Page 43

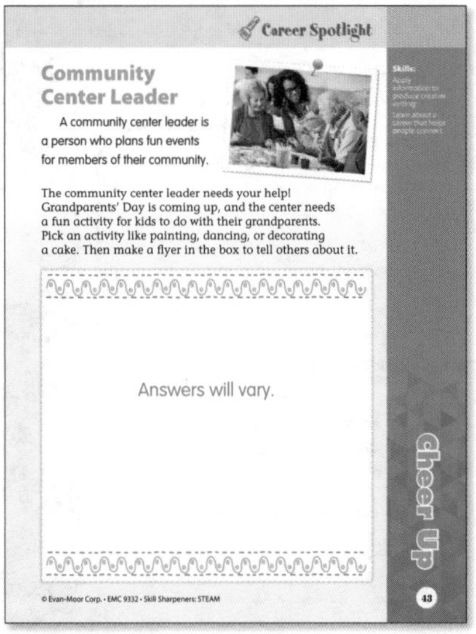
Career Spotlight

Community Center Leader

A community center leader is a person who plans fun events for members of their community.

The community center leader needs your help! Grandparents' Day is coming up, and the center needs a fun activity for kids to do with their grandparents. Pick an activity like painting, dancing, or decorating a cake. Then make a flyer in the box to tell others about it.

Answers will vary.

Cheer Up

© Evan-Moor Corp. • EMC 9332 • Skill Sharpeners: STEAM 43

Page 49

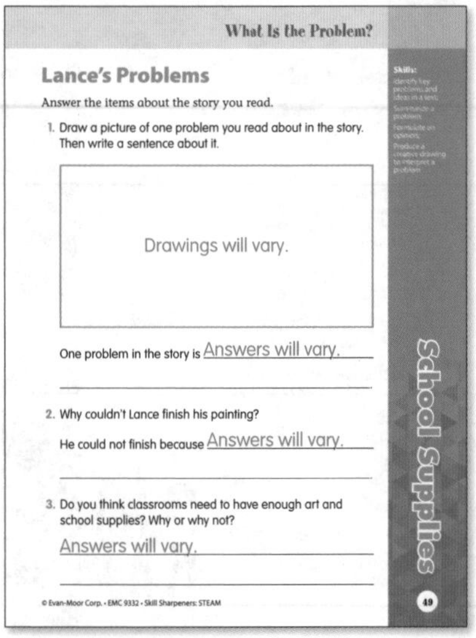
What Is the Problem?

Lance's Problems

Answer the items about the story you read.

1. Draw a picture of one problem you read about in the story. Then write a sentence about it.
   Drawings will vary.
   One problem in the story is Answers will vary.
2. Why couldn't Lance finish his painting?
   He could not finish because Answers will vary.
3. Do you think classrooms need to have enough art and school supplies? Why or why not?
   Answers will vary.

School Supplies

© Evan-Moor Corp. • EMC 9332 • Skill Sharpeners: STEAM 49

Page 55

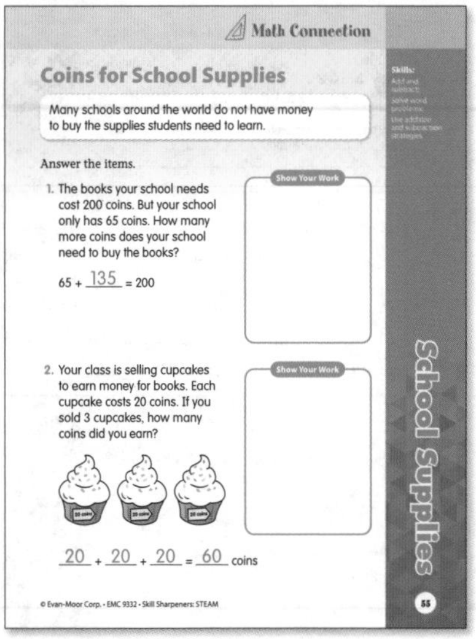
Math Connection

Coins for School Supplies

Many schools around the world do not have money to buy the supplies students need to learn.

Answer the items.

1. The books your school needs cost 200 coins. But your school only has 65 coins. How many more coins does your school need to buy the books?
   65 + 135 = 200
2. Your class is selling cupcakes to earn money for books. Each cupcake costs 20 coins. If you sold 3 cupcakes, how many coins did you earn?
   20 + 20 + 20 = 60 coins

Show Your Work

School Supplies

© Evan-Moor Corp. • EMC 9332 • Skill Sharpeners: STEAM 55

Page 56

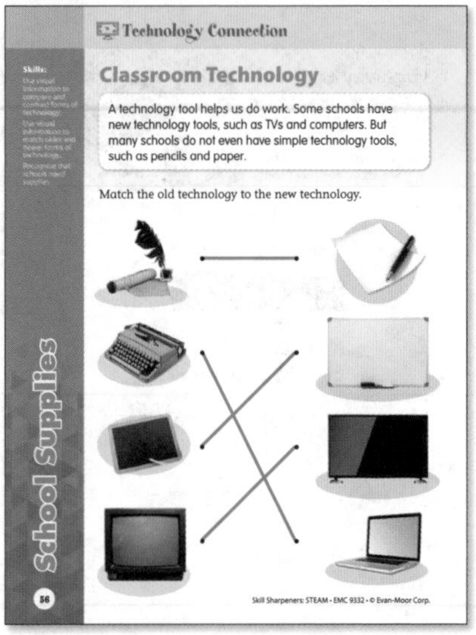
Technology Connection

Classroom Technology

A technology tool helps us do work. Some schools have new technology tools, such as TVs and computers. But many schools do not even have simple technology tools, such as pencils and paper.

Match the old technology to the new technology.

School Supplies

56 Skill Sharpeners: STEAM • EMC 9332 • © Evan-Moor Corp.

Page 57

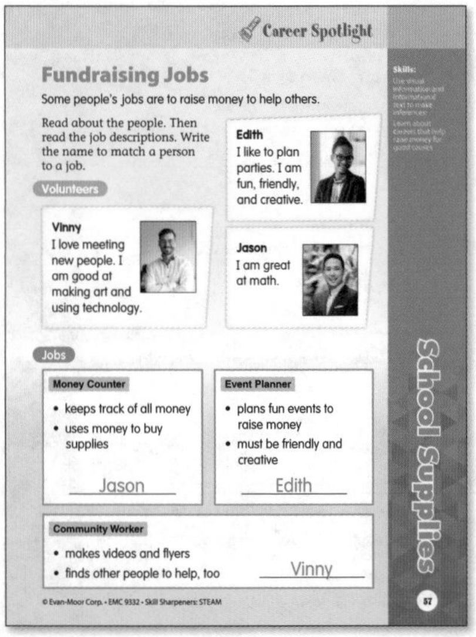
Career Spotlight

Fundraising Jobs

Some people's jobs are to raise money to help others.

Read about the people. Then read the job descriptions. Write the name to match a person to a job.

Volunteers

Edith: I like to plan parties. I am fun, friendly, and creative.

Vinny: I love meeting new people. I am good at making art and using technology.

Jason: I am great at math.

Jobs

Money Counter
- keeps track of all money
- uses money to buy supplies

Jason

Event Planner
- plans fun events to raise money
- must be friendly and creative

Edith

Community Worker
- makes videos and flyers
- finds other people to help, too

Vinny

School Supplies

© Evan-Moor Corp. • EMC 9332 • Skill Sharpeners: STEAM 57

Page 63

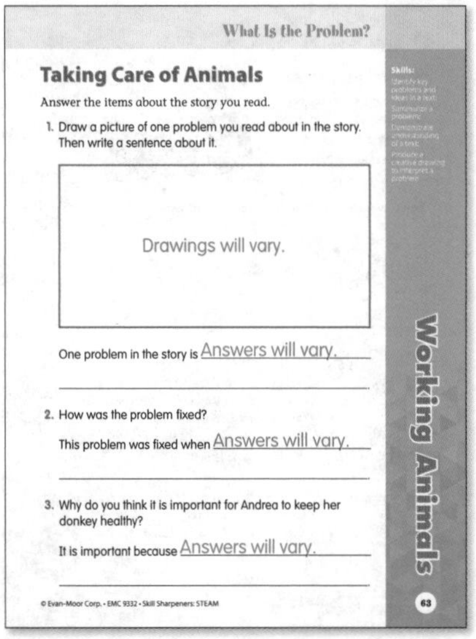
What Is the Problem?

Taking Care of Animals

Answer the items about the story you read.

1. Draw a picture of one problem you read about in the story. Then write a sentence about it.
   Drawings will vary.
   One problem in the story is Answers will vary.
2. How was the problem fixed?
   This problem was fixed when Answers will vary.
3. Why do you think it is important for Andrea to keep her donkey healthy?
   It is important because Answers will vary.

Working Animals

© Evan-Moor Corp. • EMC 9332 • Skill Sharpeners: STEAM 63

Page 69

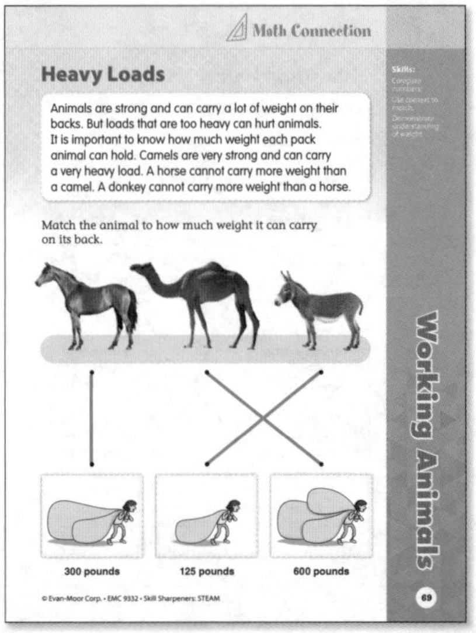
Math Connection

Heavy Loads

Animals are strong and can carry a lot of weight on their backs. But loads that are too heavy can hurt animals. It is important to know how much weight each pack animal can hold. Camels are very strong and can carry a very heavy load. A horse cannot carry more weight than a camel. A donkey cannot carry more weight than a horse.

Match the animal to how much weight it can carry on its back.

300 pounds 125 pounds 600 pounds

Working Animals

© Evan-Moor Corp. • EMC 9332 • Skill Sharpeners: STEAM 69

Page 70

Technology Connection

Animals and Technology

People use animals and technology to help them do work. Some farmers have oxen pull plows to loosen the soil on their farms. Some people use horses to pull them in wagons.

Look at the pictures. Then unscramble the word to tell which piece of technology is being used in each picture.

1. DELS — S L E D
2. LWOP — P L O W
3. GNWAO — W A G O N

Working Animals

70 Skill Sharpeners: STEAM • EMC 9332 • © Evan-Moor Corp.

Page 71

Career Spotlight

Veterinarian

A veterinarian is an animal doctor. A vet helps sick or hurt animals. A vet can tell you how to keep your pet animals happy and healthy.

Look at the picture. Read the paragraph and all of the sentences below. Then draw an **X** in the box if the sentence tells a way to help the horse be healthy.

This horse is having trouble carrying heavy loads. The horse walks very slowly and has no energy. The bottom of the horse's hooves are worn down.

- [ ] Braid the horse's hair.
- [X] Feed the horse healthy meals.
- [X] Give the horse horseshoes to protect its worn hooves.
- [ ] Make the horse work harder.
- [X] Give the horse smaller loads to carry.

Working Animals

© Evan-Moor Corp. • EMC 9332 • Skill Sharpeners: STEAM 71

Page 77

What Is the Problem?

Class Bully

Answer the items about the story you read.

1. Draw a picture of one problem you read about in the story. Then write a sentence about it.

Drawings will vary.

One problem in the story is Answers will vary.

2. How would you feel if you were Jesse?

I would feel Answers will vary.

3. What would you do if someone was bullying you?

I would Answers will vary.

Bullying

© Evan-Moor Corp. • EMC 9332 • Skill Sharpeners: STEAM 77

Page 84

Engineering Connection

A Quiet Space

Some classrooms have a quiet place where students can go when they need to take a break. Students can read books, hold stuffed animals, or do puzzles or other quiet things. If you are feeling sad, mad, or tired, going to a quiet place can help you feel better.

Help your teacher design a quiet place in your classroom. Draw a picture of what it would look like. Then finish the sentence to tell more about it.

Drawings will vary.

In the quiet place, you can Answers will vary.

Bullying

84 Skill Sharpeners: STEAM • EMC 9332 • © Evan-Moor Corp.

Page 85

Career Spotlight

School Counselor

A school counselor is a person who students can talk to when they have a problem. A counselor can help students who are being bullied, having trouble learning, or having trouble making friends.

Imagine that you are a school counselor. Fill in the circles that show how you can help when a bully hurts others.

- ● Teach a student who is being bullied how to make the bully stop.
- ○ Join the bully and tease kids together.
- ● Help the bully learn better ways to show feelings.
- ● Talk and listen to both the bully and the other student's feelings.

Bullying

© Evan-Moor Corp. • EMC 9332 • Skill Sharpeners: STEAM 85

Page 91

What Is the Problem?

Problems with Lunch

Answer the items about the story you read.

1. Draw a picture of one problem you read about in the story. Then write a sentence about it.

Drawings will vary.

One problem in the story is Answers will vary.

2. What happened that made Kapoor feel better about living in the United States?

Kapoor felt better when Answers will vary.

3. How would you feel if you could not eat the foods you like?

I would feel Answers will vary.

School Lunches

© Evan-Moor Corp. • EMC 9332 • Skill Sharpeners: STEAM 91

Page 97

Science Connection

School Lunches

A healthy school lunch has food from each of the 5 healthy food groups.

Look at the foods. Sort them into food groups. Write the name of each food on the line in its food group.

apple, carrots, chicken, bread, milk

Dairy	Vegetables	Fruits
milk	carrots	apple

Meats and Eggs	Grains
chicken	bread

School Lunches

© Evan-Moor Corp. • EMC 9332 • Skill Sharpeners: STEAM 97

Page 98

Technology Connection

Cooking with Technology

Technology can help you make different food. Pictures are a technology. Recipes sometimes have pictures to show you how to make the food. Television and videos are also technologies that you can use to watch how food is made.

Read. Look at the pictures. Number the recipe in order.

- 3 Lay vegetables, eggs, or meat on top of the rice.
- 1 Place a piece of seaweed on the bamboo mat.
- 4 Use the bamboo mat to roll your sushi. Cut and enjoy!
- 2 Spread white rice over the seaweed.

School Lunches

98 Skill Sharpeners: STEAM • EMC 9332 • © Evan-Moor Corp.

Page 99

Career Spotlight

Chef

A chef is a person who makes food. Chefs work in restaurants, hotels, schools, and many other places. A chef can cook many different foods.

Read about what people eat. Then read the menu choices. Draw a line to match each person to something he or she would like to eat.

- I like to eat spicy foods. — Jerk Chicken: Spicy chicken served with rice
- I do not eat meat. — Hummus and Pita Bread: A vegetable and bean dip with flatbread
- I love sandwiches. — Banh Mi (Baun-Me): Bread filled with fresh meat and vegetables

School Lunches

© Evan-Moor Corp. • EMC 9332 • Skill Sharpeners: STEAM 99

Page 105

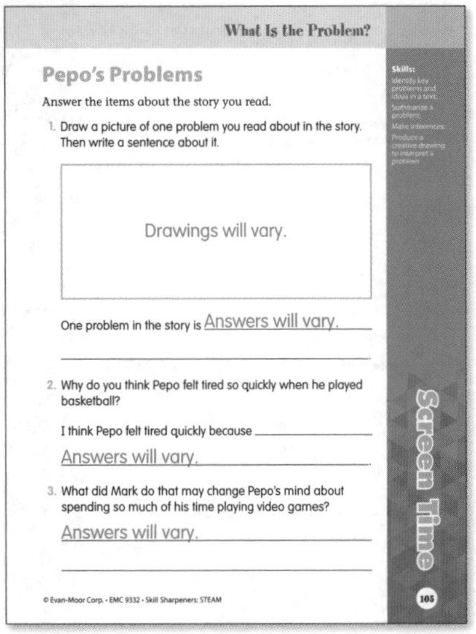
What Is the Problem?

Pepo's Problems

Answer the items about the story you read.

1. Draw a picture of one problem you read about in the story. Then write a sentence about it.

Drawings will vary.

One problem in the story is Answers will vary.

2. Why do you think Pepo felt tired so quickly when he played basketball?

I think Pepo felt tired quickly because Answers will vary.

3. What did Mark do that may change Pepo's mind about spending so much of his time playing video games?

Answers will vary.

Screen Time

© Evan-Moor Corp. • EMC 9332 • Skill Sharpeners: STEAM 105

Page 111

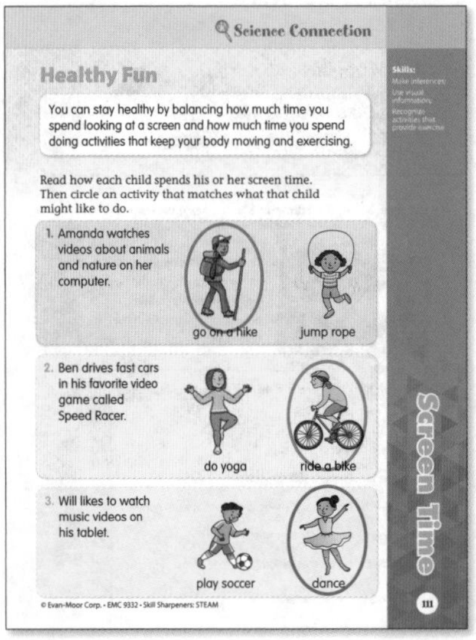
Science Connection

Healthy Fun

You can stay healthy by balancing how much time you spend looking at a screen and how much time you spend doing activities that keep your body moving and exercising.

Read how each child spends his or her screen time. Then circle an activity that matches what that child might like to do.

1. Amanda watches videos about animals and nature on her computer. go on a hike / jump rope
2. Ben drives fast cars in his favorite video game called Speed Racer. do yoga / ride a bike
3. Will likes to watch music videos on his tablet. play soccer / dance

Screen Time

© Evan-Moor Corp. • EMC 9332 • Skill Sharpeners: STEAM 111

Page 112

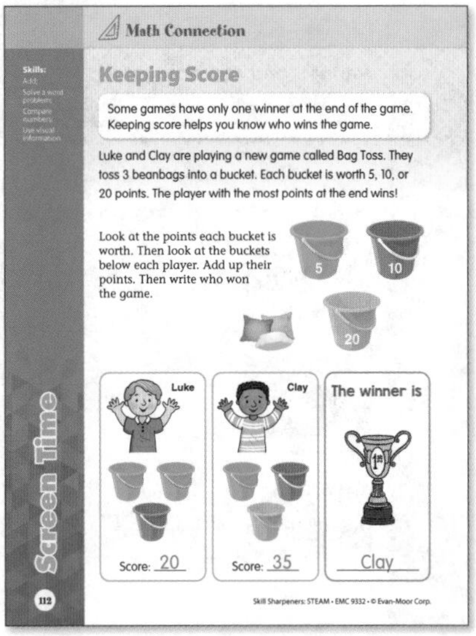
Math Connection

Keeping Score

Some games have only one winner at the end of the game. Keeping score helps you know who wins the game.

Luke and Clay are playing a new game called Bag Toss. They toss 3 beanbags into a bucket. Each bucket is worth 5, 10, or 20 points. The player with the most points at the end wins!

Look at the points each bucket is worth. Then look at the buckets below each player. Add up their points. Then write who won the game.

Luke — Score: 20

Clay — Score: 35

The winner is Clay

Screen Time

112 Skill Sharpeners: STEAM • EMC 9332 • © Evan-Moor Corp.

Page 113

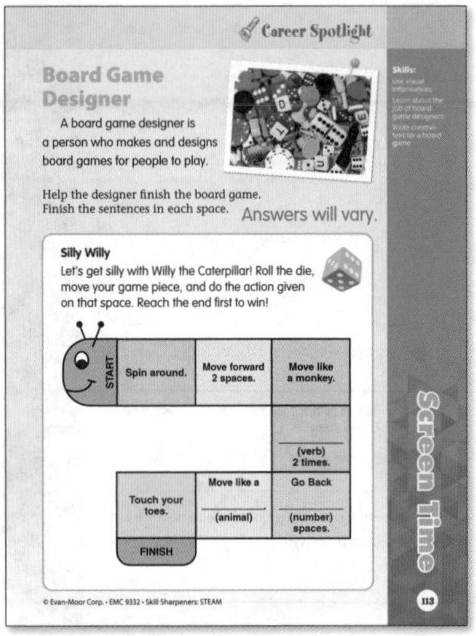
Career Spotlight

Board Game Designer

A board game designer is a person who makes and designs board games for people to play.

Help the designer finish the board game. Finish the sentences in each space. Answers will vary.

Silly Willy

Let's get silly with Willy the Caterpillar! Roll the die, move your game piece, and do the action given on that space. Reach the end first to win!

START · Spin around. · Move forward 2 spaces. · Move like a monkey. · (verb) 2 times. · Go Back (number) spaces. · Move like a (animal) · Touch your toes. · FINISH

Screen Time

© Evan-Moor Corp. • EMC 9332 • Skill Sharpeners: STEAM 113

Page 119

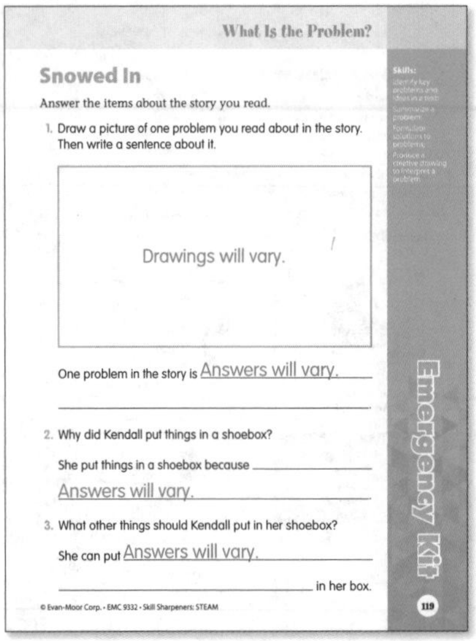
What Is the Problem?

Snowed In

Answer the items about the story you read.

1. Draw a picture of one problem you read about in the story. Then write a sentence about it.

Drawings will vary.

One problem in the story is Answers will vary.

2. Why did Kendall put things in a shoebox?

She put things in a shoebox because Answers will vary.

3. What other things should Kendall put in her shoebox?

She can put Answers will vary. in her box.

Emergency Kit

© Evan-Moor Corp. • EMC 9332 • Skill Sharpeners: STEAM 119

Page 125

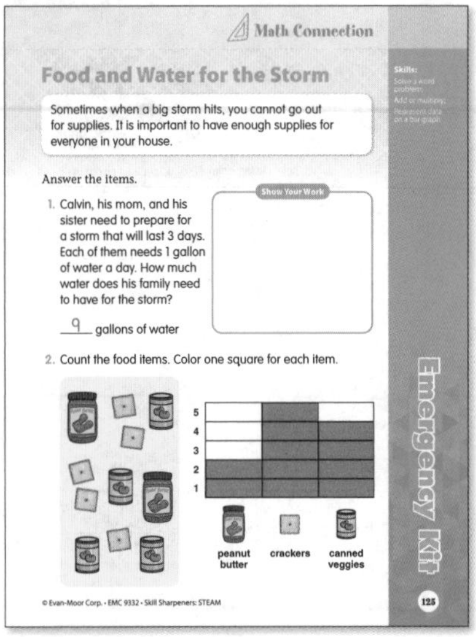
Math Connection

Food and Water for the Storm

Sometimes when a big storm hits, you cannot go out for supplies. It is important to have enough supplies for everyone in your house.

Answer the items.

1. Calvin, his mom, and his sister need to prepare for a storm that will last 3 days. Each of them needs 1 gallon of water a day. How much water does his family need to have for the storm?

Show Your Work

9 gallons of water

2. Count the food items. Color one square for each item.

peanut butter · crackers · canned veggies

Emergency Kit

© Evan-Moor Corp. • EMC 9332 • Skill Sharpeners: STEAM 125

Page 126

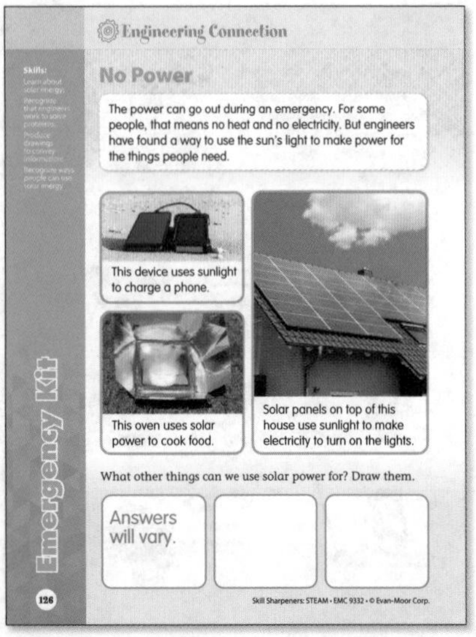
Engineering Connection

No Power

The power can go out during an emergency. For some people, that means no heat and no electricity. But engineers have found a way to use the sun's light to make power for the things people need.

This device uses sunlight to charge a phone.

This oven uses solar power to cook food.

Solar panels on top of this house use sunlight to make electricity to turn on the lights.

What other things can we use solar power for? Draw them.

Answers will vary.

Emergency Kit

126 Skill Sharpeners: STEAM • EMC 9332 • © Evan-Moor Corp.

Page 127

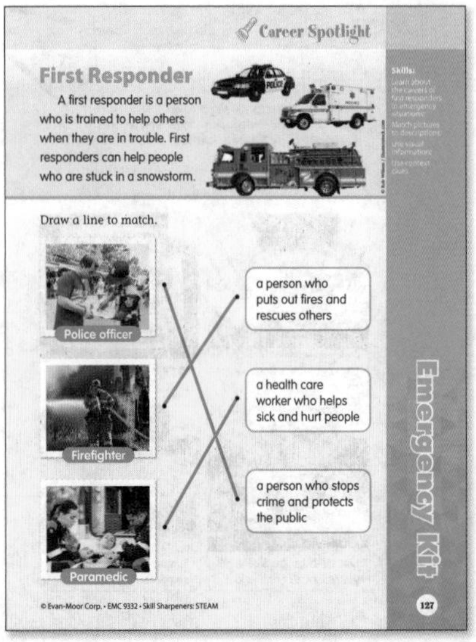
Career Spotlight

First Responder

A first responder is a person who is trained to help others when they are in trouble. First responders can help people who are stuck in a snowstorm.

Draw a line to match.

Police officer · Firefighter · Paramedic

a person who puts out fires and rescues others

a health care worker who helps sick and hurt people

a person who stops crime and protects the public

Emergency Kit

© Evan-Moor Corp. • EMC 9332 • Skill Sharpeners: STEAM 127